Berlitz

COSTA DEL SOL
and Andalusia

- A ☑ in the text denotes a highly recommended sight
- A complete A–Z of practical information starts on p.107
- Extensive mapping throughout: on cover flaps and in text

Printed in Switzerland by Weber SA, Bienne.

2nd edition
Reprinted with corrections 1996

Although we make every effort to ensure the accuracy of the information in this guide, changes do occur. If you have any new information, suggestions or corrections to contribute, we would like to hear from you. Please write to Berlitz Publishing at one of the addresses above.

Text:	Neil Wilson
Editors:	Nicola Gadsby, Delphine Verroest
Layout:	Suzanna Boyle
Photography:	Neil Wilson
Cartography:	Falk-Verlag, Hamburg
Thanks to:	The Spanish National Tourist Office for their invaluable assistance in the preparation of this guide.

Cover photograph: *Casares* © The Telegraph Colour Library

CONTENTS

The Region and the People

The Costa del Sol – Spain's Sunshine Coast – is Europe's richest, fastest-growing and most intensely developed resort area. At first sight it's difficult to see why this should be – the beaches are narrow and the sand grey and gravelly; the scenery is not particularly attractive, and scarred by cuttings for the coastal highway; and from Málaga to Marbella the concrete crush of hotels and apartment complexes runs almost unbroken. However, two features make people from all over Europe come back again and again – the magnificent climate, and the atmosphere.

Love it or hate it, the Costa del Sol is one of the liveliest and most cosmopolitan resort areas in the world. In fact, it's so cosmopolitan it's possible to forget that you're in Spain.

Yet this part of the coast lies along the southern edge of a quintessential Spanish region – Andalucía. Think of Spain and you picture bullfights, flamenco dancers, orange trees, patios hung with geraniums; all of these images are the essence of Andalucía. And therein lies the other great attraction of the Costa del Sol – only an hour's drive from the sun, sea and sangria lifestyle of the coast, you can explore the rich cultural heritage of Spain's southernmost province.

The city of Málaga is the main gateway to the Costa del Sol. The N-340 coastal highway, recently much improved, runs the length of the coast from Cádiz to Almería, linking Málaga to all the main resort centres. Protected by a screen of mountains – the Sierra Nevada to the east of Málaga, the Serranía de Ronda to the west – the Sunshine Coast suffers none of the climatic extremes of inland Andalucía. An average of 320 cloud-free days a year guarantees an enjoyable holiday – even in the depths of winter, the thermometer averages an equable 16°C (60°F), while the summer sea breezes cool the afternoon highs of 30°C (86°F) and more.

Geraniums add a splash of colour to an otherwise sober Andalucian balcony.

The eastern part of the Costa, from Málaga to Almería, is quieter and less intensively developed than the Torremolinos area. Hotels, villas and residential complexes proliferate around Nerja, the biggest resort on this stretch of coast. It pulls in more than 80,000 holiday-makers in summer, but even here some of the atmosphere of rural Spain remains. **6** Around Adra and Motril, the N-340 cuts through rich agricultural land, planted variously with avocado, citrus fruit, sugar cane, bananas and bamboo. Increasingly, you will see tower cranes sprouting along the horizon, as rising land prices to the west drive development relentlessly towards Almería.

The familiar image of the Costa del Sol, however, is to be found west of Málaga, where ribbon development backs the beaches in the original boomtown of Torremolinos. Highrise hotels and squat apartment blocks loom above the waterfront promenade, and the bustling back streets are lined with pubs, snooker clubs, discos, chip shops and curry houses.

Concrete and billboards fringe the four-lane motorway all the way to Fuengirola, Torremolinos's slightly more staid partner in grime. The apartment complexes around the marina at Benalmádena, however, are far more attractive than the unregulated sprawl of their neighbours, and show what can be achieved with a little foresight. Future growth along the coast is likely to be along these lines.

These new developments take their lead from Marbella, the original playground of the sixties' jet-set, and the upmarket showcase of the Costa del Sol. Prince Alfonso von Hohenlohe first put the town on the map back in the 1950s, and today's oil-rich Arab potentates keep it in the news. However, over the years Marbella has become accessible to far more people, and neighbouring Puerto Banús has taken over as the place to be seen. Perfectly tanned couples dripping with gold frequent the cafés, bars and restaurants along the harbourfront, where yachts from five continents lie at anchor. Puerto Banús also offers some of the most sophisticated shopping this side of St Tropez.

Towards Estepona, the hotels and apartment complexes begin to thin out, though hoardings announce building plots, marina berths and golfing villas-to-be for sale. As stretches of empty beach and green hill sides become more common, the hazy bulk of Gibraltar begins to loom, with the thin line of Africa smudging the horizon beyond. The Costa del Sol comes to an end where the highway leaves the coast and heads for the industrial towns of San Roque and Algeciras.

'The Rock' is easily accessible from all the Costa del Sol

Puerto Banús, Marbella's harbour, provides a playground for Europe's super-rich.

resorts, and a popular day trip destination. The Moors took Gibraltar in 711, the year they launched their successful conquest of Spain; seven and a half centuries would pass before Christian forces finally recaptured it. Then in 1704, the 'key to the Mediterranean' fell into English hands, and there it remains – a relic of empire, and a bone of contention between Spain and Great Britain. Spain closed its border with Gibraltar from 1969 to 1985, in the hope of forcing its return, but back in 1967 the Gibraltarians – who are not Spanish, inci-dentally, but a rich ethnic mixture of Genoese, Portuguese, Spanish, Maltese, and British blood – voted overwhelmingly for continued British sovereignty, by 12,138 votes to 44.

Within reach of the coast lie the great cities of Andalucía: Ronda, with its stunning gorge and its 18th-century bullring; Jerez de la Frontera, the headquarters of the world's sherry trade; Sevilla, famed for its April Fair and flamenco dancers; Córdoba, the grand historic capital of Moorish Spain; and Granada, city of the magnificent Alhambra palace. Tour

Lovely orange trees (naranjos) shade the streets of many Andalucian towns.

operators in the coastal resorts offer day trips to these and other destinations; alternatively, you might like to hire a car and explore at your leisure.

The abundance of international restaurants, supermarkets and fast-food franchises means that you could easily spend a fortnight on the Costa del Sol without ever tasting a real Spanish meal. Still, you shouldn't throw away the opportunity to sample the delights of Andalucian cuisine – this is the home of *gazpacho*, *rabo de toro* and *jamón Serrano*, three specialities anyone should try. And to wash down your meal, there's cooling *sangria*, now nearly as popular abroad as it is on Spain's southern shores, the sherries of Jerez, and the sweet, dark wines of Málaga.

A full calendar of festivals, pilgrimages and fairs provides added interest for the visitor.

Málaga's Holy Week processions evoke the same religious fervour as the more famous parades in Sevilla, followed soon after by the riotous *Feria de Abril*. The annual Horse Fair in Jerez celebrates Andalucía's fabled equestrian tradition.

Spring festivals in Estepona and Nerja feature costumed parades, fireworks, folk dancing and concerts. In July, all the seaside towns pay tribute to the Virgen del Carmen, the patron saint of fishermen: regattas, processions and fireworks abound. August sees a festival of music and dance in Nerja, while Málaga's fair features **9**

A merry riot of wild flowers transforms the Spanish countryside in spring.

theatrical performances and other cultural events.

In all the resorts, flamenco shows are staged for the tourists, but these are but a shadow of pure flamenco in the authentic Andalucian tradition. The outsider rarely sees the real thing, the spontaneous singing and dancing that takes place in the traditional bars and back streets of Málaga and Sevilla. But spontaneous singing and dancing of a more familiar kind can easily be experienced in the remarkable concentration of bars, night-clubs and discotheques in Torremolinos and Fuengirola, where every night is party night. Two gambling casinos operate from dusk till dawn, one in Benalmádena-Costa, the other in Marbella.

Like all Spaniards, Andalucians are a generous and tolerant people. Outnumbered by foreigners on their home territory, they take the tourist invasion in their stride, welcoming the influx of cash and the enhanced opportunities that it has brought. There have been problems, of course. Bad press in the 1980s complained of uncontrolled development, traffic congestion, dirty beaches, polluted seas and a rising crime rate. However, the complaints have been heeded, and recent years have seen a vigorous and

reasonably effective campaign to clean up the beaches and water, build better roads and by-passes, and a clamp down on crime. Competition from resorts in Greece and Turkey has forced the Costa del Sol to clean up its act considerably.

The factors that led to the Costa del Sol being developed in the first place are still a major part of its attraction – it's cheap and easy to get to,

has good beaches, and the sun can be relied upon to shine nine days out of ten. On top of that, tourists today are beginning to realise that the region has a lot more to offer than sun, sand and sangria.

So don't spend all your time on the beach – abandon the towel and the suntan lotion for a day or two, and explore a little of the Andalucía that lies hidden behind the sierras.

A Brief History

Since time immemorial, so it would seem, the southern part of Spain has been a geographical crossroads – the gateway between the Mediterranean and the Atlantic, and the crossing point between Africa and Europe. Its strategic importance has therefore given rise to a long and turbulent history.

The earliest evidence of human occupation is provided by the Palaeolithic cave paintings in the Cueva de la Pileta, some 25,000 years old.

Neolithic peoples arrived on the scene in the 4th millennium BC, leaving behind signs of early attempts at agriculture, and fragments of their pottery. Tribes of Iberians from North Africa crossed over into Spain around 3000 BC, and initiated Spain's first experiments in architecture – Spain's oldest 'building' stands near Antequera, a dolmen burial chamber known as the Cueva de Romeral. After 900 BC, wandering bands of Celts entered the peninsula from northern Europe, and brought to the area their knowledge of bronze- and iron-working. As they moved further south, they merged with the Iberians, and began to build walled villages along the coast.

Traders and Colonizers

About the same time this was taking place, the Phoenicians were already venturing across the Mediterranean from their homeland in present-day Lebanon. They reached Spain by about 1100 BC, founding many trading settlements in the 'remote' or 'hidden land' they called *Span* or *Spania*. The first was Gadir (modern Cádiz), followed by Malaka (now Málaga) and Abdera (Adra) on the Costa del Sol. Contact with the sophisticated Phoenicians introduced the Celt-Iberians to the concept of currency.

After about 650 BC, Greek traders entered the competition to exploit Spain's rich mineral deposits and fertile land. The influence of Ancient Greece, never dominant in Andalucía, was short-lived, although the olive and the grape, both Greek

HISTORICAL LANDMARKS

c. 23 000 BC	Prehistoric man inhabits caves in southern Spain.
c. 3000 BC	Iberian tribes migrate to Spain from North Africa.
1100 BC	Phoenicians found coastal settlements.
900 BC	Celts wander south from northern Europe.
650 BC	Greek traders found a series of colonies.
2nd cen. BC	Romans conquer Spain.
AD 5th cen.	Visigothic kingdom established.
711	Moors launch their conquest of Spain.
929	Caliphate of Córdoba founded.
11th-12th cen.	The caliphate splinters into small kingdoms called *taifas*. Almoravid warriors move in (1086), followed by the Almohads (1151).
1212	Christians defeat Moors at Las Navas de Tolosa.
1232	Nasrid dynasty founded in Granada.
1492	Granada falls to Ferdinand and Isabella. Christopher Columbus discovers America.
16th cen.	Emperor Charles V and Philip II expand Spain's empire during the Golden Age.
1609	The *moriscos* are expelled from Spain.
1704	Great Britain captures Gibraltar.
1808	Napoleon sets his brother, Joseph, on the Spanish throne, triggering the War of Independence (1808-14).
1902-31	Political unrest grows under King Alfonso XIII.
1936-39	Spanish Civil War.
1939-75	Dictatorship of General Francisco Franco.
1950s	Tourist boom begins on the Costa del Sol.
1975	Spain returns to democracy. Monarchy restored.
1981	King Juan Carlos helps to thwart a military coup.
1986	Spain enters European Economic Community.

legacies, soon became important, well-tended crops.

The Carthaginians, a North African people related to the Phoenicians, subsequently took over much of southern Spain, beginning with Cádiz in precisely 501 BC. They extended their influence along the River Guadalquivir to Sevilla, then to Córdoba. On the coast, they founded the city of Carteya, overlooking the Bay of Algeciras (240 BC). Fish curing sheds were set up and the trade in minerals flourished.

The North African Carthage, challenged by Rome in the First Punic War (264-241 BC), lost most of its Spanish possessions to Iberian attacks. But its fortunes changed with an initial victory in the Second Punic War (218-201 BC).

Emboldened, the Carthaginian general Hannibal decided to advance on Rome. He led one of history's great military marches from Spain into Italy, crossing the Pyrenees and the Alps on the way. The Romans invaded Spain to cut off Hannibal's supply route – and stayed **14** there for 600 years.

Roman Rule

It took the Romans two centuries to subdue the Iberians, but in the end, most of the peninsula was incorporated into their new colony of Hispania. The south formed part of the province of Baetica, virtually identical to today's Andalucía, with Córdoba its capital.

There's no doubt that the Roman presence in Spain had a far-reaching influence on the country. A road network was constructed – the Via Augusta ran the length of the south coast on its way to Rome – and bridges, aqueducts, villas and public buildings were added to the list of their achievements. Stability and a degree of unity were promoted by the introduction of the Latin language (from which modern Spanish developed), Roman law (the basis of Spain's legal system), and, eventually, Christianity.

But the Roman empire, overstretched and increasingly corrupt, began to crumble. The Romans withdrew from Spain, leaving the country to be overrun by various barbarian tribes,

An ancient Roman bathhouse on the coast, near San Pedro de Alcántara.

especially the Vandals. These tribes were eventually dominated by the Visigoths, who controlled much of southern Spain for some 300 years.

Ultimately, the Visigothic kingdom proved unstable. The monarchy was elective, rather than hereditary, which led to disputes over succession to the crown; and in one of these, the disaffected party looked to North Africa for an ally.

Moors and Christians

In AD 711, some 12,000 Berber troops landed at Gibraltar, led by the Arab chief Tariq-ibn-Ziyad. Thus began 800 years of Moorish rule – and Christian opposition. Following their victory at the Battle of Guadalete, the Moors (the name given to the Muslims in Spain) carried all before them. They pushed the Visigoths into the northern mountains, and within ten years most of the country had fallen to Islam. To this day, Almuñécar, Tarifa, Algeciras, Benalmádena and several other southern towns are known by their Arabic names. So, for that matter, is Andalucía, originally the Moorish kingdom of Al Andalus.

The Moors chose Córdoba as their seat of government, and from the 8th to 11th centuries it ranked as one of the great cities of the world, famed for its culture and erudition. **15**

Abd-er-Rahman I established the Ummayad dynasty here in 756. Thirty years later, he ordered the construction of the grand mosque, better known as La Mezquita, which remains as Córdoba's most impressive monument.

A metropolis of half a million people in its heyday, the city was capital of the independent caliphate of Córdoba, founded by Abd-er-Rahman III in 929. Under the caliphs, southern Spain knew prosperity and peace, for the Moors were relatively tolerant rulers and taxed non-believers rather than trying to convert them. Intellectual life flourished, and great advances were made in science and medicine.

With the introduction of a sophisticated irrigation system, crops such as rice, cotton and sugar cane were cultivated for the first time on Spanish soil, as well as oranges, peaches and pomegranates. The manufacture of paper and glass was another Moorish innovation.

Skilled engineers and architects, the Moors built numerous palaces and fortifications.

Superb craftsmen too, they excelled in the production of ceramics, tooled leather, as well as delicate silverware.

The ensuing fall of Córdoba was as remarkable as its rise. Early in the 11th century, the caliphate splintered into a number of small kingdoms called *taifas*, who spent their whole time warring among themselves. The Christians in the north, seeing the enemy weakened and divided, captured the *taifa* of Toledo. Under threat of attack, the other *taifas* sought help from the Almoravids, fanatical Berber warriors. The Berbers marched against the Christians in 1086, and went on to reduce Moorish Spain to a province of their own North African empire.

For a time, therefore, the affairs of Muslim Spain were administered from the Almoravid headquarters in Granada, until they lost their grip on the peninsula, softened by their life of ease in Andalucía.

The pattern repeated itself a century later when the Moors invoked the aid of the Almohads in 1151. These primitive tribesmen, who came from the Atlas Mountains of Morocco, soon made themselves the masters of southern Spain. They constructed major fortifications, such as Sevilla's Alcázar, endowing the Moors with sufficient strength to resist the Christian forces a while longer.

The fortunes of the opposing camps swayed to and fro until 1212, when the Christians gained their first decisive victory at Las Navas de Tolosa in northern Andalucía. The Christians gradually captured and annexed the former bastions of Moorish rule – in 1236 Córdoba fell to James the Conqueror, followed by Sevilla in 1248. The Moors were in retreat, retrenching along the coast and withdrawing to the security of their strongholds in Ronda and Granada.

In military disarray and political decline, Moorish Spain nevertheless saw another two centuries of brilliance under the Nasrid dynasty, founded in Granada by Mohammed I in 1232. Refugees from Córdoba and Sevilla flooded into the city, bringing with them their many talents and skills and adding to the city's brilliance.

The magnificent palace of the Alhambra provided the setting for a luxurious court life dedicated to the pursuit of literature, music and the arts.

The Jewish philosopher Maimonides (1135-1204) lived in 12th-century Córdoba.

However, the Moorish fortresses along the coast soon came under attack. Sancho IV took Gibraltar in 1310, but the Christians later relinquished their prize, and the Moors held on to it until 1462. Then, in the 1480s, the Christians launched a new offensive – Ronda capitulated to the sovereigns Ferdinand and Isabella in 1485, followed by Málaga in 1487 and Almería in 1488.

All Christendom gave thanks when Granada was conquered at last in 1492. That same year, Christopher Columbus discovered the New World in the name of the Spanish crown. A new era had begun.

The Golden Age

With the triumph of Christianity, the country was united under the 'Catholic Monarchs' (*Los Reyes Catolicos*), a title conferred by Pope Alexander VI on Ferdinand II of Aragon and Isabella I of Castile. Fanatical in their religious zeal, in 1492 the king and queen expelled all Jews who refused to convert to Christianity, followed by the Moors in 1502. In so doing, they reneged on the promise of religious freedom they had given when Granada surrendered. With the Jews who left Spain went many of the country's bankers and merchants, and with the Moors, a good number of its agriculturists and labourers.

The converted Jews (*conversos*) and Moors (*moriscos*) who remained in Spain were viewed with suspicion by the Inquisition, which had been established by the Catholic Monarchs to stamp out heresy. Many were condemned to death, and still more fled the country to escape persecution.

The 16th century was glorious for Spain. The conquest of the New World brought prestige and wealth. Sevilla, the port of departure for the Americas, had a monopoly on trade with Spain's territories there, granted by Queen Isabella. For over two centuries, no city in the country was richer.

By comparison, the coastal settlements languished, subject to frequent raids by Barbary pirates. The king ordered the construction of a chain of watch-towers along the coast, but he was powerless to stop the pirate attacks. Under constant threat for more than 200 years, the population drifted inland, taking refuge in fortified towns and villages hidden in the foothills of the sierras. Rumour had it that the *moriscos* passed intelligence to the pirates; they were also suspected of abetting the Turks, the new rising power in the Mediterranean.

As Emperor Charles V of the Holy Roman Empire, the Spanish king turned his attention to events in Europe. Between 1521 and 1556, he went to war with France four times, squandering the riches of the Americas on endless military campaigns. Charles also had a weakness for costly architectural projects like his vast Renaissance palace in the grounds of the Alhambra, which he

The military exploits of Emperor Charles V are recorded in his palace in the Alhambra.

19

commissioned in 1526. Taxes imposed on the Moors served to finance the building works, which eventually had to be abandoned for lack of funds when the *moriscos* revolted 12 years into the reign of Philip II (1556-1598). The king dispatched his half-brother, Don Juan of Austria, to quell the rebellion, which ended in 1570 with the defeat of the *moriscos* and their eventual dispersal.

The rout of the Turkish fleet at Lepanto the following year left Spain in control of the Mediterranean, but its dominance was short-lived. In 1588 Philip II made ready to invade England, only to be repulsed when the English navy destroyed Spain's invincible Armada. The defeat marked the start of a long, slow decline.

Philip's military forays and his expensive taste left Spain encumbered with debts. Participation in the Thirty Years' War under Philip III led to further financial difficulties and another debacle – Spanish troops were defeated by the French at Rocroi, in Flanders (1643), never to regain their prestige.

French Ascendancy

Spain's internal affairs became the concern of the other great powers after Charles II died without an heir. The Archduke Charles of Austria challenged France's Philip of Bourbon in the ensuing War of the Spanish Succession. Gibraltar was the scene of some fierce fighting in 1704, when Great Britain captured the Rock on behalf of its ally, Austria. Unable to oust the British, Spain was finally forced to relinquish its claims to Gibraltar in 1713, under the terms of the Treaty of Utrecht, which also confirmed Philip's right to the Spanish throne.

Nearly a hundred years later, during the Napoleonic Wars, Spanish ships fought alongside the French fleet against Lord Nelson at Cape Trafalgar (see p. 47). But as the wars continued, Napoleon, distrustful of his ally, forced the Spanish king Ferdinand VII to abdicate in 1808, and imposed his brother, Joseph, as king. He then sent thousands of troops across the Pyrenees to subjugate the Spaniards, who promptly revolted.

Aided by British troops subsequently commanded by the Duke of Wellington, the Spanish drove the French out of the Iberian peninsula. At Tarifa, the enemy was defeated literally overnight in an offensive of 1811. What the world now knows as the Peninsular War (1808-14) is in fact referred to in Spain as the War of Independence. Indeed, during this troubled period, the country's first, short-lived, constitution was drafted, and the Spanish colonies of South America won their independence.

Troubled Times

Ferdinand's return to the throne in 1814 destroyed any hopes for a constitutional monarchy, while tension between liberals and conservatives led to a century of conflict, marked by the upheavals of the three Carlist wars and the abortive First Republic, proclaimed in 1873.

On the Andalucian coast, the 19th century was a time of tentative expansion. With piracy at an end (see p. 18), a number of towns and villages grew up along the shoreline, and the extension of the railway line to Almería in 1899 promoted the early development of the eastern region.

Alfonso XIII, a young man of only 16, assumed the crown in 1902. His reign was a difficult time for Spain; prosperity and stability eluded the country, which remained neutral during World War I.

Against a murky background of violence, strikes and regional strife, the king accepted the dictatorship of General Miguel Primo de Rivera in 1923. Seven years later, the opposition of radical forces toppled Primo de Rivera from power. Neither reform nor the maintenance of order seemed possible. Alfonso XIII went into exile following anti-royalist election results in 1931, and another republic was founded.

Parliamentary elections in 1933 resulted in a swing to the right, as public opinion became polarized. When the left came out on top in the elections of 1936, the situation deteriorated at an alarming rate. It came as no surprise, when, **21** six months later, General Francisco Franco led a large section of the army against the socialist government.

Support for the Franco-led Nationalist uprising came from monarchists, conservatives, the right-wing Falangist organization, as well as the Roman Catholic Church, while liberals, socialists, communists and anarchists sided with the government. Right from the outset, the Civil War assumed an international character, involving as it did Germany and Italy on the Nationalist side, with Russia and the volunteers of the International Brigade backing the Republicans.

The bloodshed lasted no less than three years and cost hundreds of thousands of lives. General Franco emerged as the leader of a shattered Spain. Many Republicans went into exile; others simply disappeared. The Republican mayor of Mijas caused a sensation when he finally surfaced in the 1960s after three decades in hiding – in his own home.

Franco kept Spain out of World War II, despite Hitler's entreaties to the contrary. Nor did Gibraltar participate actively in the conflict. The Spanish nation slowly, gradually healed its wounds, though conditions in the country were difficult and life was far from easy.

Changing Fortunes

All that was to change, virtually overnight, as Spain's tourist potential began to be exploited in the 1950s. The government made credit available for the development of hotel complexes and apartment blocks in coastal areas, including the Costa del Sol.

Soon, fishing villages like Torremolinos and Marbella began to sprout sprawling concrete suburbs, and the boom began in spectacular fashion, gaining momentum with the admission of Spain to the United Nations in 1955. The advent of jet travel and package holidays in the 1960s opened up the coast to mass tourism, with profound consequences for the economy and the people.

With the death of General Franco in 1975, Spain returned

to democracy. In accordance with Franco's wishes, the monarchy was restored in the person of King Juan Carlos, the grandson of Alfonso XIII (see p. 21). More than just a figurehead, the king helped to thwart a military coup in 1981, keeping Spain firmly on a democratic course.

The socialist government of Felipe Gonzalez was elected in 1982, and committed itself to Spain's successful integration into the European Community. As a precondition to admission, the border with Gibraltar was re-opened in February 1985, after a 16-year hiatus, and Spain was admitted to the EC in 1986. Despite high unemployment figures and separatist rumblings, the country's economy remained one of the fastest-growing in Western Europe throughout the 1980s.

The golden year of 1992 – when Madrid was crowned cultural capital of Europe, Barcelona hosted the Olympic Games, Sevilla staged Expo 92, and the whole nation celebrated the 500th anniversary of Christopher Columbus' discov-

*S*pain's King Juan Carlos is a popular figure in his own country as well as around the world.

ery of the New World – put Spain on the front page all over the world. The Costa del Sol can only benefit from the afterglow of all that publicity – it looks like Spain's Sunshine Coast will continue to shine for many years to come. **23**

Where to Go

Most visitors to the Costa del Sol will be based in one of the large coastal resorts – Nerja, Torremolinos, Fuengirola, or Marbella – travelling from there to see the sights in Málaga, and perhaps making an excursion to Gibraltar, and a side trip or two to Ronda and the mountains. The more adventurous will want to go farther afield, to Sevilla, Córdoba and Granada – tour operators offer popular one-day coach excursions to these destinations.

Renting a car and driving to The Rock of Gibraltar for the day is quite feasible, but going to Sevilla and back in one day really isn't practical – to get the most out of the more dis-

---

Costa del Sol Highlights

MARBELLA OLD TOWN: centred on its old church tower, a maze of narrow streets filled with little shops and cafés.

GIBRALTAR: the Rock of Gibraltar, a British colony since 1713, has several famous sights – the Apes' Den, Upper Galleries, and views across the strait to the coast of Morocco.

RONDA: a fortified hilltop town divided by the spectacular Tajo gorge and linked by an 18th-century bridge. There are many walks in the area.

SEVILLA: Capital of Andalucía, with a fine Gothic cathedral, Moorish Alcázar, and historic Barrio Santa Cruz district. Home of flamenco, bullfighting and the colourful Feria de Abril.

CORDOBA: once a Moorish capital, one of the medieval world's most important cities; famous for its mosque, La Mezquita.

GRANADA: home of the magnificent hilltop Alhambra Palace, in a wonderful setting at the foot of the Sierra Nevada mountains.

*M*álaga's Moorish fortress rises beyond the colourful town-hall gardens.

tant destinations, you do need to stay overnight.

Our tour of the coast begins in the gateway city of Málaga, site of the Costa del Sol's international airport. After a look at the major monuments and museums, we head west along the N-340 to Torremolinos, Benalmádena and Fuengirola, and up into the hills to Mijas. Back on the coast, we continue through rather exclusive Marbella and terribly smart Puerto Banús, Nueva Andalucía and San Pedro de Alcántara, then it's on to Algeciras and Tarifa via Estepona, San Roque, La Línea and Gibraltar.

Eastwards from Málaga, we make for the Nerja holiday resort, and on to the Almuñécar beach development and Salobreña, past Motril and Adra to journey's end – the cathedral city of Almería, at the eastern limit of the Costa del Sol.

Málaga

For tourists from the cosmopolitan beach resorts along the coast, Málaga offers a refreshing taste of the real Spain. There are twisting, narrow streets, shady public gardens, an old Moorish fortress and a waterfront promenade, with plenty of traditional *tapas* bars, cafés, and nightlife – and of course bullfights.

The city looks back on more than 3,000 years of history. **25**

Founded by Phoenician traders, it came under Carthaginian and Roman rule before falling to the Moorish invasion force in 711. The Moors fortified the city, developing the settlement into a major trading port serving Granada. Málaga remained a Moorish stronghold for centuries, but fell at last to Christian forces in 1487. It took 60,000 men and three months of siege to force a surrender.

Spread around the hill of Gibralfaro – Málaga's principal landmark – the city sprawls between the sierra and the sea. With a population of half a million, it's a sizeable metropolis, but nearly everything of interest to the visitor lies within the maze of streets in the old quarter. The easiest way to see the sights is to take one of the coach excursions offered by travel agencies in the resorts. It requires stamina to trek round the city in the heat of summer – especially on the climb up the Gibralfaro – and to cope with the chaotic traffic at any time of the year. Remember that Málaga slumbers through the siesta hour –

from around 1.30 to 4 or 5pm (see p.89) – so plan ahead, and do your sightseeing and shopping in the morning or late afternoon.

City tours take in the cathedral, bullring and Gibralfaro area, with a stop at a *bodega*, or wine cellar, to sample Málaga's famous sweet red wine. If you can find time for a return visit, don't miss the fascinating folk art museum, housed in an old inn, and the Museum of Fine Arts, with early paintings by the town's most famous native son, Pablo Picasso.

CITY SIGHTS

A good place to begin your tour of Málaga is at the top – some 130m (425ft) above the city on the summit of the pine-clad **Gibralfaro** (from the Arabic *Jebel al Faro* – Lighthouse Hill). A road takes cars and coaches all the way to the top; the more energetic can climb a footpath from the gardens above the Town Hall (but avoid this path after dark).

The hilltop is capped by the ramparts of a Phoenician castle reconstructed in the 14th century by the Moors, who went on to build the lighthouse which gave Gibralfaro its name. The restored walls and parapets offer a superb view of Málaga and its surroundings – from the bullring just below you, across the harbour and east to the sandy sweep of Málaga beach. On a clear day you can look across the city centre all the way to Fuengirola, 30km (18 miles) to the west. Just below the castle is the Parador Málaga-Gibralfaro, a small hotel with a fine situation (see p.68).

Finding Your Way Around

alcazaba	fortress	jardín	garden
alcázar	castle citadel	mercado	market
		mezquita	mosque
ascensor	lift, elevator	muelle	docks
autopista	motorway, highway	murallas	ramparts
		museo	museum
avenida	avenue	oficina de turismo	tourist office
ayuntamiento	town hall		
barrio	quarter	paseo	boulevard
cabo	cape	playa	beach
calle	street	plaza	square
carretera	road	plaza de toros	bullring
castillo	castle		
ciudad vieja	old town	puerto	harbour
correos	post office	río	river
cueva	cave	sierra	mountain range
estación de ferrocarril	railway station	vía	avenue
faro	lighthouse	derecha	right
fortaleza	fortress	izquierda	left
iglesia	church	todo derecho	straight ahead
isla	island		

27

The childhood home of Pablo Picasso has been turned into a small museum.

records some of the more thrilling moments in the history of the *corrida* (bullfight).

Created on reclaimed land, the **Paseo del Parque** parallels the waterfront. Luxuriant palm and plane trees, bougainvillaea, aloes and geraniums flourish in this seaside tropical garden. Midway along the avenue, past the Town Hall (*Ayuntamiento*) and post office (*correos*), Plaza de la Aduana gives on to the **Alcazaba**, the sprawling fortress that made the city a stronghold of the Moorish kingdom of Al Andalus. Beside the entrance lie the partially excavated ruins of a Roman theatre, the only visible remains of the ancient city.

A cobbled path climbs up the hillside within the walls to the portal dubbed Arco del Cristo (Gateway of Christ). The victorious Christian army of Ferdinand and Isabella cel-

On your way back to town you may want to take a closer look at Málaga's colonnaded 19th-century **bullring** (*plaza de toros*). When bullfights are held, crowds of 14,000 gather to watch the heirs of Joselito and Manolete perform their 'ballet of death' in the arena (see p.94). For real fans, a **28** small museum on the premises

ebrated mass here when the fortress finally fell into their hands in 1487. Higher still, the one-time palace of the Moors contains a museum of classical and Islamic artefacts, including fragments of Roman statues and Hispano-Moresque pottery.

The partially restored palace will prove a let-down to anyone who expects a little Alhambra, but the view from the ramparts doesn't disappoint – like Málaga's Moorish rulers, you look down on a breathtaking panorama of sky and sea, with the whole city spread at your feet.

Paseo del Parque comes to an end at the open space of Plaza de la Marina. Here Calle de Molina Lario leads past the Hotel Málaga Palacio to the **cathedral**, known locally as *La Manquita* – the one-armed lady – because one of its twin towers remains unfinished. The north tower soars 100m (some 330ft) high above the street, but work on the other, a forlorn stump of stone, stopped in 1783 through lack of money.

Málaga was the birthplace of Pablo Ruiz Picasso, though the young artist left his native city at age 14 for the more cosmopolitan climates of Madrid and Barcelona. The **Museo de Bellas Artes** (Fine Arts Museum), around the corner from the cathedral in Calle de San Agustin, preserves some of the furniture from the Picasso family home (still standing at Plaza de la Merced 15, and now housing a museum of its own), as well as works by the young Picasso and his first teacher, Antonio Muñoz Degrain. The precocious *Los Viejos* (The Old Couple), produced at the age of ten under Muñoz's tutelage, already shows signs of genius. Apart from the Picassos, the museum displays paintings and sculpture by Luís de Morales, Murillo (a spiritual *Saint Francis de Paula*), Alonso Cano (an intense *Saint John the Evangelist* stands out) and Pedro de Mena, with special emphasis on the masters of the 19th-century Málaga school. Recently renovated, the building itself is of interest; the old Renaissance-style palace encloses pleasant courtyards bedecked with flowers. **29**

A city of commerce as well as culture, Málaga offers shopping of a traditional nature along three main thoroughfares: Molina Lario, Calle de

Scrubbing the decks at the marina in Benalmádena-Costa.

Marqués de Larios (completely rebuilt after the Civil War), and the pedestrian Calle de Granada. You can buy almost anything here, from foodstuffs to footwear. This is also the place to sample some of Málaga's sweet red wines, the speciality of the house in the many bars and *tabernas* that dot the neighbourhood.

The residents of Málaga's historic town centre shop daily for food in the century-old **mercado central** (central market). You enter through a Moorish arch that is a relic of the old city walls. Though the ramparts of brick are gone, the bazaar atmosphere of the *zoco* (the market-place of the Moors) lives on, as butchers, fishmongers, greengrocers and spice sellers all vie for customers. The stalls display the bounty of Málaga's hinterland – pyramids of oranges and almonds, slabs spread with sea bass, swordfish and clams, thick braids of garlic, strings of sausage, and fragrant bouquets of wild thyme.

The **Museo de Artes y Tradiciones Populares** is a charming little folk art museum installed in a historic inn of 1632, the Posada de la Victoria. It lies at the western edge of the old town on the bank of the Guadalmedina, Málaga's sluggish river. The exhibits take you back to the time before the tourist boom, when the resorts were small fishing villages and people made a living from the sea alone. Retired from use not so very long ago, an old forge and a bakery with millstone and wood-burning oven, a *bodega* (wine cellar) and printer's workshop all make fascinating tableaux. There's an array of popular ceramics on display, as well as some appealing rustic furniture (notice the well-used birth chair).

AROUND MÁLAGA

Just an hour's drive north of Málaga lies some magnificent mountain scenery. The national park of **El Torcal de Antequera** is a high limestone plateau that has been eroded by rainwater into a fantasy landscape of fluted pinnacles and towers. Hikers can explore the waymarked trails, which are up to 5km (some 3 miles) in length, winding among the rocks, and enjoy panoramic views back to Málaga and the distant blue Mediterranean.

Near the town of Alora you will find the breathtaking gorge known as the **Garganta del Chorro**; this 300m (1,000ft) deep, sheer-sided canyon is cut by the Guadalhorce River (also accessible from Málaga by train – ask for a ticket to El Chorro). An improbable concrete catwalk called the Camino del Rey (The King's Way) crosses a vertical cliff and continues into the heart of the gorge, a dizzying 65m (200ft) above the river. It was built in the 1920s to provide access for workers digging tunnels for a hydroelectric scheme. Today the walkway is in a highly dangerous state of disrepair – don't even think about trying it! The artificial dams above the gorge have created attractive lakes – the **Pantanos del Chorro** – fringed with woods, sandy beaches and campsites, a refreshing change from the heat and bustle of the coast. **31**

West to Tarifa

West of Málaga, some of the world's most popular beach resorts line the 162km (100-mile) stretch of coast to the Rock of Gibraltar. If it's nightlife you're after, you'll enjoy the lively bars and clubs of Torremolinos; Fuengirola is more family-orientated, with the emphasis on shopping and beach life. Marbella and Puerto Banús are more stylish and upmarket resorts, with brand new marinas, several excellent golf courses and exclusive restaurants, while Estepona and the newer developments further west are quieter and tend to be less crowded.

TORREMOLINOS

Nearest to Málaga lies Torremolinos, the brash, cosmopolitan capital of the Costa del Sol. Love it or hate it, there's no denying that it delivers everything a sun-hungry holiday-maker could wish for in the way of beaches, restaurants, bars, pubs, discotheques and nightclubs, with all the com-

forts of home thrown in for some visitors – British pubs, British breakfasts, British newspapers and magazines. There are also German pubs, Danish pubs, Dutch pubs, Swedish pubs, and even Icelandic pubs! In fact, in Torremolinos, you can hear just about every European language under the sun – except Spanish.

At the town centre is the busy Plaza Costa del Sol and the neighbouring **Calle San Miguel**, with its much-photographed profusion of shop signs. At the bottom of San Miguel, a flight of steps leads down towards a 10km (6-mile) sweep of narrow beach, broken only by the rocky promontory of Castillo de Santa Clara, which separates the Bajondillo (east) and Carihuela (west) sections of town.

A dozen or more *chiringuitos* – simple eating houses that serve as impromptu beach clubs – overlook the Bajondillo beach, chock-a-block with basking bodies in high season.

But the most lively beach restaurants lie around the point in the former fishing village of

La Carihuela. There are still a few bona fide fishermen about, and if you can manage to drag yourself out of bed between six and eight in the morning you'll see them returning to shore in their gaily painted, flat-bottomed wooden boats, landing sardines and anchovies by the netfull. At lunchtime, you can sample the morning's catch, skewered on a wooden stick and grilled over a fire on the beach (see p.102).

Many other popular attractions lie close at hand, including the wave pools and water slides of **Atlantis Aquapark** (see p.92) and the 18 hole course of the Parador del Golf. But the biggest draw in Torremolinos continues to be the bars, discos and clubs in the town centre and along the Montemar Avenue that have earned the resort its international reputation for non-stop nightlife.

It's worth taking the time to explore some of the attractive, quiet backstreets in the older part of town, if only to remind yourself that you are indeed still in Spain.

BENALMÁDENA

The concrete towers of Torremolinos merge seamlessly into those of neighbouring **Benalmádena-Costa**. With one of the Costa del Sol's two casinos – Casino Torrequebrada, right on the N-340 – golden sands that stretch for 9km (5 miles), and a modern and attractive marina development, this resort ranks high in the popularity league. Scattered among the hotels and holiday flats are three Moorish watch-towers, standing beside the sea like outsize chess pieces. Extensive Roman ruins, still under excavation, lie to the east of the Torre Quebrada.

Well endowed with bars, discos and clubs, though less frenetic by night than Torremolinos, Benalmádena-Costa also offers some cultural diversions. Concerts and exhibitions take place within the pink, Neo-Moresque walls of **Castillo El Bil-Bil**, built by a Frenchwoman in the 1930s. The coastal highway goes right by this highly visible raspberry-pink pile, topped with a **33** crenellated tower. Inquire about activities and events in the tourist office, situated in the castle's gate-house.

A couple of kilometres inland lies the pleasant village of **Benalmádena-Pueblo**, high above the sea, with its own small bullring and sober whitewashed church. A *mirador* overlooks the terraced hillsides that slope steeply down to the teeming coastal strip.

Benalmádena-Pueblo has an institution of national importance in its **Museo de Cultura Precolombina**. Some of the Neolithic exhibits were recovered in caves around Benalmádena; the Roman artefacts were discovered along the coast. But the museum gives pride of place to a collection of Precolumbian art said to be the most important of its kind in Spain, with jewellery, statuary and ceramics from all the major cultures and periods.

Also in the Benalmádena area are the **Tívoli World** amusement park, in the suburb of Arroyo de la Miel (see p.92) and the **Sea Life** aquarium in Puerto Marina.

FUENGIROLA

Nine kilometres (6 miles) down the line, Fuengirola provides British sun-seekers with all the comforts of home. Bacon and eggs, darts and snooker, fish and chips, and flat brown beer are all easily available for those who want them. Fuengirola is somewhat less lively than Torremolinos, though far from staid, and a holiday here does come a little cheaper than in Torremolinos or Marbella. The attractions include a variety of watersports, a marina and fishing harbour, a sailing school, and the waterslides of the Mijas Aqua Park.

The Plaza de la Constitución in the town centre has numerous pleasant cafés lining the square beneath the church bell-tower. Nearby are the town's own bullring (bullfights are held here between March and October), and the small **Zoo Municipal**. This eclectic collection of lions, emus, gibbons, zebras and other species was started by a local animal lover some years back and will delight young children.

*F*lowers and candles decorate a roadside shrine in Fuengirola (above), whilst fun is in order at Mijas Aqua Park (left).

Against all the odds, a few vestiges of village life survive in Fuengirola. The commercial fishing fleet is still a going concern, and the traditional Tuesday morning **market** (called *mercadillo*) still takes place in the market place (*recinto ferial*) a few blocks east of the tourist **35**

*F*resh country produce on display at Fuengirola's mercadillo, the town's Tuesday market.

There is a Sunday market too; you'll find it in the grounds beside the marina.

Across the river at the west end of town rise the remains of the **Castillo de Sohail**. Abd-er-Rahman III built this hilltop fortress in the 10th century, and gradually a settlement grew up around the walls. Taken by the Christians in a bloody battle of 1487, Sohail was then levelled on the orders of the Catholic Kings. Rebuilt, it was occupied by French troops during the Peninsular War, who left behind a souvenir of their stay – the cannons that are now displayed along the promenade of the **Paseo Marítimo**.

MIJAS

Eight kilometres (5 miles) inland from Fuengirola lies the attractive hill village of **Mijas**. It's hardly a typical Spanish village, but don't let that keep you away. Beneath the tourist trappings the spirit of Andalucía survives. Surrounded by modern villas and *urbanizaciones* (developments) the heart of the village preserves

office on Avenida Jesus Santos Rein. You can stock up on fresh fruit, vegetables, herbs and spices, and shop for clothes and souvenirs. Tour operators all along the coast feature a weekly excursion to the Fuengirola market, usually combined with **36** a visit to the village of Mijas.

steep streets of whitewashed houses, lined with a plethora of bars, restaurants and shops, shops, shops… Traffic is banned from the centre – *burro* 'taxis', colourfully caparisoned beasts of burden, will ferry you from the car park up to the plaza beside Spain's only square **bullring**. Said to be the oldest arena in the country, it dates back to Moorish times.

Opposite the bullring, beautifully tended gardens slope down to a clifftop **mirador** (lookout), with fine views all along the coast. While you're enjoying the panorama, don't be surprised if a hand suddenly reaches up from below and grabs the railings at your feet – the cliff face beneath the gardens is a popular playground for local rock climbers, whose antics compete with the view for the attentions of visiting photographers.

There is another mirador beside the car park. On one side of this natural balcony you will find a tiny **chapel** dedicated to the Virgen de la Peña (Our Lady of the Mountain).

It is set in a grotto carved from living rock.

Inevitably, a visit to Mijas involves a quick round of the best stocked souvenir shops on the coast, overflowing with woven goods, esparto grass

The hill village of Mijas is a popular destination for day-trips from the coast.

products, tooled leather and ceramic articles of all kinds. If you have the time, try to stay for dinner in one of the many attractive restaurants around the main square.

MARBELLA

The aristocrat of Costa del Sol resorts, Marbella can boast the greatest concentration of luxury hotels in the whole of Spain. This privileged strip of coast, sheltered by the mountains of the Sierra Blanca, is the playground of the rich and famous, celebrities and politicians, royalty and business tycoons. Prices are much higher here than in the other coastal resorts, but you get what you pay for in superior standards of accommodation, service and cuisine, as well as a superb range of recreational facilities, and some of the most sophisticated shopping in Spain.

It's only appropriate that a queen should have given the town its name. When she first saw the coast here, Isabella of Castile is said to have exclaimed '¡Qué mar tan bella!'

('What a beautiful sea!'). The pragmatic Phoenicians had given their original settlement the rather more prosaic title of Salduba (Salt City).

The municipality of Marbella encompasses some 28km (17 miles) of beach front, lined with exclusive hotel complexes like Los Monteros, Puente Romano, and the resort's original development, the Marbella Club. Built in the 1950s by Prince Alfonso von Hohenlohe, the hotel launched Marbella as a trendy gathering place for the sixties' jet-set. Today the town still draws an upmarket crowd, and each summer the local population of 87,500 is quadrupled by the massive influx of visitors.

Marbella turns its most attractive face to the sea. Down by the water, a promenade swings past the beaches of El Fuerte and Fontanilla, and a **marina** (*Puerto Deportivo*) with moorings for several hundred pleasure boats, overlooked by the tall spire of the lighthouse. Some lively beach bars and restaurants make this a popular part of town.

The shapely peak of 'La Concha' (The Seashell) overlooks Marbella beach.

The promenade extends west for a mile or two, between attractive apartment complexes and long stretches of golden sands. Even the beach showers have a touch of class – the water sprays from the trunk of a fibreglass elephant!

The centre of modern Marbella, clustered around the palm trees and fountains of the Parque de la Alameda, is taken up with busy sidewalk cafés, smart boutiques, banks and estate agents' offices. The construction of a new four-lane bypass has happily put an end to the crush of traffic that regularly used to jam the resort's main avenue.

North of the main road, the **Casco Antiguo** (Old Town) provides further attractions for visitors. Here in the leafy **Plaza de los Naranjos** (Square of the Orange Trees) you can nurse a coffee at leisure, while you admire the noble 16th-century façade of the **Casa Consistorial** (Town Hall), or simply watch the people passing by. Small shops and galleries are scattered throughout the maze of narrow, twisting streets all around, the white-washed walls decorated with colourful baskets of flowers. As you explore the neighbourhood, you'll come across the historic parish church with its landmark bell-tower, and the convents of La Trinidad and San Francisco (it is said that **39**

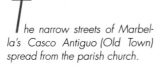

The narrow streets of Marbella's Casco Antiguo (Old Town) spread from the parish church.

Miguel de Cervantes, author of the famous *Don Quixote*, lodged at the latter). Uphill from the church lie the crumbling walls of the Moorish **castillo**.

The monuments of modern Marbella cling to the hills on the western outskirts. The

King of Saudi Arabia's holiday home – it looks like the White House in Washington DC, only slightly larger – hides behind a row of pines and palms on a hilltop just above the highway, surrounded by high security fences.

On a neighbouring rise stands Marbella's modernistic **mosque**, the Mezquita del Rey Abdulaziz Al Saud, which is open to the public every afternoon except Friday. Non-Muslims of both sexes are admitted to the serene, green-carpeted interior – but you should dress respectfully, with long trousers or a skirt, and remove your shoes before entering.

The increasing popularity of Marbella has seen the focus of high society move west to the very chic suburb of Nueva

Andalucía, and especially its magnificent harbour, **Puerto Banús**. Sleek, impossibly expensive boats line the quayside, and Bentleys, Porsches, Rolls Royces and Mercedes adorn the streets. There's a glamorous line-up of expensive restaurants and high-class boutiques – open evenings, weekends and holidays in the high season. High-rollers haunt the tables in the Nueva Andalucía Casino until dawn, then sip martinis and watch the sun rise from the after decks of their luxury yachts. Even if you can't quite afford to join in, it's fun to buy an ice cream and wander along the waterfront, counting the Cartier and Rolex wristwatches.

At the western edge of Marbella lies the golfer's paradise of **San Pedro de Alcántara**, with at least half a dozen quality courses in close proximity. This was the site of the Roman colony of Silniana, destroyed by an earthquake in the 4th century AD. Some fine mosaic pavements have been uncovered north of the town, and the remains of Roman baths and an early Christian basilica lie just south of the motorway at Guadalmina.

Inland from Marbella lie the high peaks of the **Sierra Blanca**, the most distinctive being 'La Concha' (The Seashell), which rises directly above the town. A scenic road leads to the village of Ojén (famous for its *aguardiente*, a kind of brandy) and on to the mountain pass called Puerto de Ojén. Just beyond, a road on the left leads to the **Refúgio de Juanar**, a hunting lodge set in the heart of a large national game reserve. This is the haunt of mountain hare, partridge, and the ibex or *Capra pyrenaica*, a wild mountain goat with large horns, unique to Spain.

The Juanar lodge makes an ideal base for hiking excursions in the heart of the Sierra Blanca. Once the domain of the Marquesses of Larios, the lodge is now owned and operated as a cooperative venture by the villagers of Ojén, who can arrange for guided tours, horses and hunting permits. Contact the local tourist office for more details. **41**

TOWARDS GIBRALTAR

The last major resort town on the western part of the Costa del Sol, **Estepona** provides all the holiday essentials – good beaches, golf courses, restaurants and a marina – in an engaging small-town atmosphere. Low-rise apartment blocks, unpretentious restaurants and hotels overlook the palm-lined **Paseo Marítimo**, a promenade furnished with park benches, flower displays and a little playground. Fishermen still gather to drink in the backstreet bars, and there are traditional cafés where you can enjoy a traditional breakfast of *churros y chocolate*.

Originally a Roman settlement, Estepona preserves the remains of Moorish fortifications and watch-towers, an 18th-century parish church, and an expressionistic bullring, a startling piece of modern architecture which is beginning to look rather the worse for wear. Estepona has another claim to fame in Costa Natura, a naturist resort on the western outskirts of town that happens

The 'White Town' of Casares sits precariously atop an impregnable crag.

to be the only one of its kind on the Costa del Sol.

Beyond Estepona, development is more sporadic, though there are the beginnings of two luxury resorts at Sotogrande and Puerto Duquesa. About 6km (4 miles) out of town, a mountain road takes you up to **Casares**, a spectacular white hilltop village clinging precariously to the rugged slopes below its Moorish fort.

The road commands sweeping views of the coast and countryside, and on a clear day the eye is inevitably drawn to the twin peaks flanking the Straits of Gibraltar – The Rock of Gibraltar on the right, and Morocco's Jebel Musa on the left. This is the western extremity of the Mediterranean – Monte Hacho (in the Spanish enclave of Ceuta, on the Moroccan side) and Gibraltar were known to the ancients as the

'Pillars of Hercules', and in ancient times marked the limits of the known world.

Gibraltar looms ever larger as you approach **San Roque**, established by Spanish refugees who fled the Rock when the English captured it in 1704. Building blocks for the town were found conveniently to hand in the nearby ruins of Roman Carteya; consequently, little remains of the classical site. To the south lies the border town of **La Línea**, which has experienced a mini-boom since the border with Gibraltar was re-opened in 1985 after a blockade lasting 16 years.

Gibraltar is only two hours' drive from Málaga, and makes a popular day trip from the Costa del Sol resorts. Border formalities are minimal, especially if you have a British passport. If you arrive by car, leave it in one of the car parks in La Línea and cross the border on foot – it's much faster, and once you're inside, a car is a hindrance. Beyond the customs control, walk across the middle of the airport runway; pass through the defensive walls to reach the town centre.

The name Gibraltar is a corruption of the Arabic *Jebel al-Tariq*, 'The Mountain of Tariq', **43**

after one Tariq-ibn-Ziyad, the Moorish chief who captured the Rock in 711 and used it as a bridgehead for his invasion of Spain. It was retaken by the Spanish in 1462, but in 1704 Sir George Rooke took possession for the British; it became a Crown Colony in 1830.

The town and harbour lie on the east slope of the Rock, overlooking the bay, with the narrow defile of **Main Street** cutting through the middle. The street is lined with duty-free shops selling alcohol, perfumes, cameras, CD players, video recorders and electrical goods, and British-style pubs serving pints of bitter and bar lunches. (The unit of currency is the Gibraltarian pound, which is equal to the British pound, though shops and other businesses will accept pounds sterling and pesetas as well.)

Turn right at Bomb House Lane to reach the **Museum**, which houses an interesting selection of exhibits on Gibraltar's history. Main Street ends at the Referendum Gates; beyond lies the **Cable Car Station**, where you can take a trip to the top of the Rock, with a stop halfway to visit the **Apes' Den**. The tailless Barbary apes which inhabit the Rock are natives of North Africa, descended from monkeys brought over by sailors as pets and ships' mascots. Legend has it that if the apes ever leave the Rock, then British rule will come to an end. When the apes' population declined significantly during World War II, Winston Churchill himself was worried, and the monkeys have been on special rations ever since.

The views from the summit (426m, 396ft) are spectacular, across the Straits to Morocco, along the coast towards Estepona, and down the sheer east face of the Rock to the water catchment areas and the beaches of Sandy Bay, Catalan Bay and Eastern Beach. South of the Upper Station is **Saint Michael's Cave**, an impressive natural grotto, which is sometimes used as the venue for musical performances.

You can walk from the Upper Station to the north end of the Rock, and explore the **Upper Galleries**, a system of

$\mathcal{G}$ibraltar's limestone peak rises to a height of 426m (1,396ft); it has been the object of much dispute over the centuries.

tunnels blasted through the inside of the rock face during the late 18th century, with gun emplacements overlooking La Línea. Tableaux inside explain the history of the tunnels. Below lies the **Moorish Castle**, with its 14th-century tower.

Algeciras, just across the bay from Gibraltar, offers unsurpassed views of the Rock. From the harbour, hydrofoils and car ferries cross the Strait to Ceuta, a Spanish possession, and to Tangier in Morocco. Day trips to Ceuta and Tangier (see the BERLITZ TRAVEL GUIDE TO MOROCCO) can be arranged through travel agents in major resorts or from Algeciras port.

The Costa del Sol comes to an end at **Tarifa**, where the waters of the Mediterranean mingle with the Atlantic, and Europe looks across the waves to the coast of Africa – the Rif Mountains of Morocco hang on the horizon a mere 13km (8 miles) away. In 711, the Berber warrior Tarif-ibn-Malik captured Tarifa for Islam, thus giving the town its name. A section of the old Moorish walls still stands, along with

the 10th-century fortress. Recaptured by Christian forces in 1292, it's now known as the **Castillo de Guzmàn el Bueno**, after Alonso Pérez de Guzmàn, who sacrificed the life of his own son rather than surrender to the infidel. Now occupied by the Spanish military, the castle is open to tourists at weekends only.

This pleasant town, and the beaches stretching to the west, are a Mecca for windsurfers and speed lovers, as it is one of the windiest spots in Europe – the prevailing wind is from the west, and is called the *Poniente*; its easterly counterpart is known as the *Levante*.

The windsurfers are not the only ones to take advantage of the reliable breeze – the hillsides above the town have sprouted a veritable forest of wind-powered electricity generators. In spring and autumn, storks, buzzards and other soaring birds fill the skies as they climb in the rising thermals before gliding across the Straits on their annual migration, congregating here where the sea-crossing is at its shortest.

East to Almería

The eastern part of the Costa del Sol stretches for over 200km (125 miles) from Málaga to Almería. This part of the coast has a different feel to the western section, with less intensive development and a rockier shoreline. Emerging from the suburbs of Málaga, you arrive immediately in Rincón de la Victoria, a Spanish resort largely given over to weekend flats owned by the local city dwellers. But prehistoric man was here first – he occupied a cave on the Málaga side of the town known as **Cueva del Tesoro** (Treasure Cave). According to legend, five Moorish kings buried a huge treasure inside the cave, but it has never been found.

High-rise Torre del Mar is the gateway to the wine- and raisin-producing region of the Axarquía, and its capital, **Vélez-Málaga**, a town of 30,000 inhabitants which lies 4km (2½ miles) inland. Founded by the Phoenicians, Vélez sprawls around a historic centre dominated by a Moorish *alcazaba* and two venerable churches – the Late-Gothic Iglesia de San Juan Bautista, and the Iglesia de Santa María, which incorporates a section of the town's former mosque.

The Battle of Trafalgar

Fifty kilometres (30 miles) north west of Tarifa lies the Cabo de Trafalgar (from the Arabic *Tarif al-Gar*, or Cape of the Cave). Off this headland, on 21 October 1805, a British fleet of 27 ships under Admiral Horatio Nelson engaged a combined French and Spanish fleet of 33 ships in one of history's most famous naval battles, which established Britain's naval supremacy for the next 100 years. At the end of the day, the enemy was routed, losing nearly two-thirds of its ships. No British vessels were lost, but Nelson was hit by a sniper's bullet, and died just before the battle's end.

The Balcón de Europa over-looks Nerja's La Caletilla beach.

The coastal villages of Mez-quitilla, Lagos and El Morche woo tourists with numerous tennis courts, swimming pools and the obligatory *discoteca*. Here as elsewhere on the east-ern Costa, self-catering accom-modation predominates over hotels and *hostales* (modest hotels). Once dedicated solely to fishing and agriculture, Tor-rox-Costa is now an expanding resort. Apartment complexes

have sprung up alongside the extensive Roman ruins – a lighthouse, baths, and a fish-curing house.

NERJA

There's just one big interna-tional resort to the east of Málaga, and that's **Nerja,** a popular destination for British, German and Scandinavian hol-iday-makers. The town (popu-lation 30,000) is smaller than the big resorts to the west, with less intensive high-rise devel-opment, and has also managed to retain some of its village atmosphere. The nightlife is lively, though less so than in Torremolinos, and the beaches are prettier, but smaller, being squeezed into rocky coves. The area offers good opportu-nities for hiking, horse-riding, scuba diving, snorkelling and angling, giving Nerja the edge for those seeking a more active holiday, while the annual festi-val of music and dance is an added cultural attraction. Ho-tels and restaurants cluster around the **Balcón de Europa**, a palm-fringed cliff-top promenade jutting out over the sea, dividing the sandy crescent of La Caletilla beach on the west from La Calahonda on the east. Nerja has a good number of other beaches, but the best are **Playa de Burriana**, beneath the Parador Nacional, just east of town, and **Maro**, 6km (4 miles) further on. Nerja's lively restaurants and bars – many of them owned and operated by resident foreigners – form one of the resort's greatest attractions. The odd *burro* plods through the streets, carrying building materials or vats of wine, and old women stand gossiping in the doorways.

Just outside Maro is the famous **Cueva de Nerja** (Cave of Nerja). This huge cavern was discovered relatively recently, in 1959, when a group of local boys stumbled on it one day while they were out hunting bats. Floodlights illuminate the impressive limestone formations, including a stalagmite/stalactite which is said to be the world's largest. As you enter the cave you will probably be startled by a flash of light as the local photographer takes your picture – it will be developed and printed by the time you come out, but you are under no obligation to buy a copy. On display in the first chamber are photographs of prehistoric wall-paintings discovered in the cave (but not yet on view to visitors), some fragments of pottery, and human bones of prehistoric vintage. (Occupied as early as 20,000 years ago, the cave was inhabited intermittently until about 1800 BC.) During the Nerja Festival, held annually around the middle of August, concerts are performed inside the main chamber.

Inland from Nerja, the corrugated hills of the Sierra de Tejeda rise up towards the village of **Frigiliana**. Under the Moors, Frigiliana was one of the many prosperous villages within the Kingdom of Granada. Today the historic centre is regarded as one of the most outstanding examples of Moorish village architecture on the Costa del Sol, with a lovely 16th-century church and ruined Moorish castle lending some added atmosphere. **49**

Climb up the wide, cobbled steps to the **mirador** for a stunning view over the village, its whitewashed houses surrounded by an apron of terraced fields, and down to Nerja and the sea below.

A patchwork of small farms and terraced fields covers the countryside around Nerja.

THE FAR EAST

The pace of development is picking up now that road improvements have been made on the eastern reaches of the N-340. From Nerja, the highway weaves through the mountains, with views of rocky coves and crumbling Moorish watch-towers. The views of the ragged coastline are magnificent (surpassed only by the panorama from the old road that snakes up precipitously to the **Cerro Gordo** lookout). Some 20km (12 miles) from Nerja, La Herradura's highrise beachfront and the smart resort community of Punta de la Mona bring you back to civilization with a jolt.

Further along the coast, the attractive beach development of **Almuñécar** lies beneath the old town, inviolate atop its small hill. A port for Granada in Moorish times, Almuñécar continued to enjoy a certain prestige after the Reconquest – Juan de Herrera, the architect of El Escorial, Philip II's grand palace near Madrid, was commissioned to design the parish church, and its bell-tower is the work of Diego de Siloé.

To get a feeling for the place, climb up through the narrow, dusty streets of the Barrio San Miguel to the **Moorish castle**. With land inside the walls at a premium, the pragmatic people of Almuñécar long ago turned the courtyard of the fort into a cemetery. Almuñécar has always been famous for its red pottery, and you can still see artisans at work here, turning out all manner of traditional pieces. Just outside town, a fine **aqueduct** stands as a monument to the skills of the Roman engineers who constructed it during the reign of Antoninus Pius in the 2nd century AD.

A scenic corniche road leads on for another 15km (9 miles) or so, through barren, undulating hills, devoid of all vegetation. As the coast flattens out, the white-walled town of **Salobreña** comes into view. Built on a rocky outcrop surrounded by yellow-green fields of sugar cane, the village makes an impressive sight. A Moorish fortress, beautifully restored, is Salobreña's crowning glory,

while outside the walls, modern resort hotels sweep along 3km (2 miles) of beachfront.

Industry takes precedence over tourism in the thriving port city of **Motril**. Sugar cane flourishes in the surrounding *vega* (plain), and the abundant sugar refineries in the town have earned it the nickname 'Little Cuba'. However, pleasant beaches lie near at hand in Torrenueva, Calahonda and Castell de Ferro. Beyond the city, the road deteriorates into a narrow, twisting switchback following the tortuous shoreline, and plagued by slow-moving lorries weighed down with their heavy cargoes.

A dreary, barren stretch of coastline, where every available piece of level land has been covered in agricultural plastic (this particular area produces much of Europe's winter vegetables), leads to the important fishing and fish processing centre of Adra. To the east lie the expanding luxury resorts of Almerimar, Roquetas de Mar and Aguadulce, with good beaches, new golf courses and marinas. **51**

ALMERÍA

A city rich in history and tradition, Almería was once the most important city in Moorish Spain. In its heyday in the 11th century, its early importance gave rise to the Spanish saying 'When Almería was Almería, Granada was but its farm'. The Almería of today is a pleasant provincial capital of 200,000 inhabitants, worth a visit should your travels take you to the eastern limits of the Costa del Sol – a distance of 222km (138 miles) from Málaga.

There are only two major sights. The forbidding, fortified **cathedral** stands just inland from the waterfront Paseo de Almeria. Built during the 16th century, when Barbary pirates were terrorizing the coast (see p.18), this bastion of the faith helped to bolster Almería's seaward defences.

Abd-er-Rahman III's massive **Alcazaba** looms large on the hilltop above the city. Although an earthquake caused extensive damage in 1522, the crenellated ochre outer walls and a section of the turreted ramparts stand firm, providing wide-ranging vistas over the city and the sea. (It is not advisable to visit the Alcazaba alone, especially at night, as there may be thieves around.)

Inland from Almería lies one of the most un-European landscapes in all of Europe. The **Sierra de Alhamilla** is a desert of barren mountains, rocky ravines and dry gravel river beds, with spiky agave plants and prickly pear as the only vegetation. Its uncanny resemblance to the American West made it a popular film location for spaghetti westerns, including such classics as *A Fistful of Dollars* and *The Good, The Bad, And The Ugly*, which set a young Clint Eastwood on the road to stardom in Hollywood. Parts of *Lawrence of Arabia* and *The Man Who Would Be King* were also shot here.

Near the village of Tabernas is an area known as **Mini Hollywood**, where two spaghetti western film sets have been preserved as tourist attractions, complete with horses, cowboys and bar-room brawls.

Excursions Inland

For a complete contrast to the sun, sea and sangria atmosphere of the coast, you need only drive inland for a few hours to reach the cultural, historical and architectural attractions of Ronda, Jerez, Sevilla, Córdoba, and Granada – the great cities of Andalucía. If your time is limited, try one of the day trips which are offered in all the major resorts.

RONDA

The opening of an improved road from San Pedro de Alcántara to Ronda has ended the isolation of this mountain redoubt, and shortened the driving time from the coast to an hour. One of the most spectacularly situated towns, Ronda sits atop a cliff-bound plateau, cleaved through the middle by a sheer-sided gorge. The older, Moorish part of town (*La Ciudad*) lies to the south of the defile, linked by an 18th-century bridge to El Mercadillo, the modern district that sprang up following the Reconquista.

The gorge, known as **El Tajo**, is a deep and narrow ravine that plunges 150m (490ft) to the foaming Río Guadalevín, a tributary of the Guadiaro. During the Civil War, Nationalist sympathizers in the town were hurled to their deaths in the gorge, an event recalled by Hemingway in his novel *For Whom the Bell Tolls*. You can enjoy a superb view of the Tajo and the patchwork of fields beyond from the **Puente Nuevo** (New Bridge), built in 1788.

Cross the bridge into the **Ciudad**, the old Moorish enclave, which remained impervious to Christian assault until 1485. Bear to the right and continue along to **Plaza de Campillo**, another fine vantage point. Out in the distance, you will see vultures tracing slow, menacing circles above the grey, stony ridge of Ronda's mountain range, the Serranía de Ronda. A path here leads down to the Arco de Cristo, an old Moorish gateway, where you have a fine view of the Puente Nuevo from below, and continues down to the meadows beneath the cliffs.

53

*R*onda's Puente Nuevo spans the spectacular gorge of El Tajo.

On one side of the square stands the **Palacio de Mondragón**, the one-time residence of Ronda's Moorish kings – and later, of its Christian conquerors. A Renaissance portal – a distinguished later addition – opens onto spacious courtyards where horseshoe arches, Arabic inscriptions and distinctive tile ornament indicate the Moorish origins of this grand building. Some of the rooms are out of bounds to visitors, but you can visit the garden with its spreading pomegranate tree, and the roof terrace where the Moorish ruler once gazed out across his fertile farmlands.

A street or two away, Ronda's original mosque survives as the church of **Santa María la Mayor**. The minaret was converted into a bell-tower, and a Gothic nave was tacked on to the original structure, followed later by a high altar in ornate 16th-century Plateresque style, and some finely carved Baroque choir stalls. The church overlooks the cypress-shaded expanse of the Ciudad's main square, the Plaza de la Duquesa de Parcent.

Heading back towards the Puente Nuevo, stop off at the **Palacio del Marqués de Salvatierra**, a Renaissance mansion still occasionally used by the aristocratic Salvatierra family. Guided tours begin at half-hourly intervals, morning

coals and placed under a long-skirted table, the device then warmed the lower extremities of those who sat around it; brandy presumably took care of the rest of the body.

Beyond the house, the road curves down towards the Tajo, where two more bridges span the gorge – the **Puente Viejo** (Old Bridge), built in 1616 on top of Roman foundations, and the Moorish **Puente San Miguel**. Both offer striking views of the chasm. Down by the river stand the **Baños Árabes** (Moorish Baths), with their vaulted roof still intact.

and afternoon, except when the family is in residence. As you approach, you can't help but notice the curious carved stone figures above the entrance. They are Inca Indians, a reminder that the house was built during the era of discovery and conquest of the New World. Another token of those momentous times is a carved doorway within, which bears likenesses of the great explorers, Columbus and Pizarro.

As you pass through the richly appointed rooms, the guide will point out traditional pieces of furniture like the *vargueño*, or fall-front desk, with intricate marquetry detail, and the *brasero* that served as a portable heater. Filled with hot

Back across the Puente Nuevo in the **Mercadillo** (market) is Ronda's neoclassical **Plaza de Toros**, one of the oldest bullrings in Spain. Inaugurated in 1785, it is regarded as the birthplace of the modern bullfight, and is something of a shrine to aficionados of the *corrida*. A small museum below the arcaded arena recalls the fabulous careers of the Romero family and their 20th-century successors, the Ordóñez clan.

South west of town, a scenic route leads 25km (15 miles) **55** through the fissured limestone hills of the Serranía de Ronda to the **Cueva de la Pileta** (follow the signs to Benoaján), a deep cave once inhabited by prehistoric man. A guide equipped with a lantern conducts visitors through the galleries that stretch for over a mile into the mountainside. It's a good idea to bring along a torch of your own, to illuminate better the prehistoric art work on the walls. Paintings of a bull's head and a pregnant mare are among the oldest images. Realistically rendered in ochre and black, they date back 25,000 years to Palaeolithic times.

JEREZ DE LA FRONTERA

The name of this town tells you two things: 'de la Frontera' means that it once lay close to the frontier of the old Moorish kingdom of Granada; and 'Jerez' (pronounced khay-

reth) gave its name to the wine that has made the town famous, better known to the world in its anglicized version – sherry. *Bodegas* (wineries) are the prime raison d'être of Jerez de la Frontera, and also the chief reason for visiting.

There are over 200 *bodegas* in this city of 200,000 people, among them the premises of prestigious old firms such as Garvey, Williams & Humbert, Gonzalez-Byass, and Pedro Domecq. As some of the names imply, it was a group of English merchants who launched

*A*zulejos and bodegas are among the attractions for visitors to Jerez de la Frontera.

Jerez as the world capital of fortified wine. Three centuries on, their descendants continue to control the sherry trade.

All the larger companies offer **tours** of their *bodegas* on weekday mornings; some require you to reserve in advance. At Pedro Domecq they're proud to show off casks with historic associations – both Lord Nelson and the Duke of Wellington drank the Domecq brand. Traditional hospitality means of course that every tour ends with a tasting session.

Jerez is also famous for its horses. (The sherry producing aristocracy set itself up on vast ranches, alongside the vineyards, providing an ideal environment for horse-breeding.) And indeed, the world-famous **Real Escuela Andaluza del Arte Ecuestre** (Royal Andalucían Riding School) was established in 1973 by the Domecq family as a showcase for Andalucian equestrian skills. If you can't be in Jerez for the Horse Fair in early May, try to see one of the school's Thursday dressage exhibitions.

Among the other tourist attractions, Jerez's hill-top **Alcázar** stands out. Surrounded by gardens, the fortress rises high above the town square, the Plaza de los Reyes Catolicos. Alfonso X stormed the citadel in 1264, and from that time forward Jerez remained firmly in Christian hands. Below the Alcázar lies the **Colegiata** (Collegiate Church), a towering dark stone building dating from the 17th-18th century. Housed within is the precious image of *Cristo de la Viña* (Christ of the Vineyard).

57

SEVILLA

Capital of Andalucía, home of flamenco, cradle of the *corrida*, Sevilla is the most Spanish of Spanish cities – sensual, spiritual and romantic. Amerigo Vespucci and Ferdinand Magellan set out on their epic voyages from this port. Christopher Columbus lies buried here, and it is the birthplace of two of Spain's greatest artists, Velázquez and Murillo. Bizet's *Carmen* is set in Sevilla, as is Mozart's *Marriage of Figaro*. And two of Europe's best-known festivals take place here each spring, with the religious fervour of the Holy Week parades followed a few weeks later by the *Feria de Abríl*.

Sevilla (population 700,000) was already a thriving riverside settlement when Julius Caesar arrived in 45 BC. Under the Romans, the village developed into a major town. Capital of the Visigoths, and then of a Moorish *taifa*, Sevilla finally fell to King Ferdinand III in 1248. A monopoly of trade with the New World brought **58** the city to its peak during the Golden Age. 'Madrid is the capital of Spain', the saying went, 'but Sevilla is the capital of the world.'

The Río Guadalquivir cuts a wide swathe through the city centre, separating the monumental and commercial districts on the left bank from the gypsy quarter of Triana on the right. If your time in Sevilla is limited, concentrate on the highlights – the cathedral, La Giralda and the Alcázar – clustered around the Plaza del Triunfo on the east bank.

The largest Gothic church in the world, Sevilla's **cathedral** is an architectural colossus – only St Peter's in Rome and St Paul's in London are bigger. In 1401, the city's great mosque was razed to make way for a Christian church, and the city fathers declared: 'Let us build a cathedral so immense that everyone, on beholding it, will take us for madmen.' The new building followed the ground plan of the old mosque, accounting for its unusual broad, rectangular form.

Massive without, and richly decorated within, the cathedral

The Gothic pinnacles of Sevilla's cathedral overlook the alleyways of Santa Cruz.

contains over 30 chapels, including the central **Capilla Mayor** with its huge Flemish altarpiece, and the grandiose **Capilla Real** (Royal Chapel), last resting place of Ferdinand III, the 'King-Saint' who delivered Sevilla from the hands of the infidel. The silver-gilt key to the city, presented to Ferdinand by the vanquished Moors, may be seen in the treasury, along with a cross made of the first gold brought back by Columbus from the New World. The Great Navigator himself is interred nearby, in the ornate 19th-century sarcophagus by the south entrance. His remains were transferred to Sevilla from Havana in 1898, when Cuba won its independence from Spain.

On the north side of the cathedral lies the **Patio de los Naranjos** (Court of the Orange Trees), the ceremonial courtyard of the old mosque, complete with its original ablutions fountains. The minaret was preserved as the bell-tower of the cathedral – the celebrated **Giralda**. Three sections merge harmoniously – the sober 12th-century stonework at the bottom supports a course of decorative brickwork, which is in turn capped by an ornate Renaissance bell chamber.

Sevilla's most famous landmark, the 98m (322ft) tower takes its name from the statue **59**

*T*he narrow back streets of the Barrio de Santa Cruz are lined with charming little hotels.

of *Faith* pivoting above it; the figure serves as a weather vane (*giraldillo*). Follow the ramp up to superb views of the town and its river. You can climb to the top via a cobbled ramp that spirals up inside the tower – Ferdinand III rode his horse to the top following the Reconquista in 1248.

Avenida de la Constitución leads north from the cathedral to the pedestrianized shopping district, which is centred on the

Calle de las Sierpes. East of the church lies the **Barrio de Santa Cruz**, the old Jewish quarter. This picturesque maze of white houses, narrow lanes and tiny shaded patios invites a leisurely exploration.

South of the cathedral in Plaza del Triunfo stands the former exchange building, Casa Lonja. Documents relating to the discovery and conquest of the Americas are on display.

The **Alcázar** (entrance on far side of the square, through the Puerta del León) is a major monument to mid-14th century Mudéjar architecture, combining Moorish, Gothic and Renaissance elements. Built by Moorish craftsmen under Christian rule, during the reign of Pedro the Cruel, the rambling palace and its several courtyards incorporate fragments of an earlier Moorish fortress, and blend Christian motifs with Moorish designs.

A visit begins with a tour of the Cuarto del Almirante (the Admiral's Apartments), where a painting of the Virgen de los Mareantes (Virgin of the Mariners) in the chapel shows

Columbus sheltered beneath the Virgin's cloak. The most interesting part is the Patio de las Doncellas (Courtyard of the Maidens), where the rooms preserve outstanding decorative features – ornamental tiles, carved stucco work and characteristic coffered *artesonado* ceilings. The ornate, domed **Salón de Embajadores** (Hall of the Ambassadors), is equal to anything in the palace of the Alhambra. Next door is the glass-roofed Patio de las Muñecas (Courtyard of the Dolls), so named for the two tiny human faces carved into the decoration surrounding one of the Moorish arches – exceptional, as Muslim craftsmen were forbidden by their religion to depict the human form.

Returning to the entrance courtyard, take the narrow passage on the right to the Patio de Maria Padilla, which sits on top of underground baths. The apartments beyond are hung with Flemish tapestries recording Charles's Tunis Expedition of 1535, one of them showing an upside-down map of the Mediterranean.

The Moorish **Torre del Oro** (Tower of Gold) stands down by the river. Gold-coloured tiles once covered the walls of this 13th-century chess-piece castle, all that remains of Sevilla's mediaeval fortifications. Pedro the Cruel used the

A tranquil pond reflects the Moorish architecture of Sevilla's Alcázar.

tower as a prison; now it houses a maritime museum.

Upstream from the city centre, on the far bank, lies the Cartuja, the site of the 1992 World Exhibition. A futuristic footbridge gives access to the grounds of the **Parque de los Descubrimientos** (Discovery Park), where landscaped gardens compose the setting for the pavilions that formed the centrepiece of Expo 92. The exhibits record the achievements of the great navigators and explorers, and look towards future advances in technology. Other attractions include a lakeside show, a night parade, daily circus shows at the auditorium, a fun fair, cinema, theatre and music events, and monorail and cable car rides.

CÓRDOBA

Twentieth-century Córdoba is a minor provincial city of considerable charm. It is hard to imagine that 1,000 years ago it was the splendid capital of the western Islamic empire, the

centre of the great mediaeval Caliphate of Córdoba, one of the world's largest and most cultured cities, with a population of half a million. Before the arrival of the Moors, Córdoba had been the largest city in Roman Spain, the capital of the province of Baetica, birthplace of Seneca the Younger, philosopher and tragedian.

The one surviving monument to the Ummayad dynasty is the Great Mosque of Córdoba, known as **La Mezquita**. Abd-er-Rahman I erected the original shrine in the year 785, but it was enlarged three times before attaining its present extent under Almansor in 987.

No structural changes were made when the Christians first took over, but preservation of the architecture became a major issue in the 16th century after plans were announced to raise a cathedral within the mosque. Córdoba's townspeople threatened workmen involved in the project with death, and Charles V himself was called on to officiate in the dispute. The emperor approved the construction of the cathedral, but on seeing the finished work, he deeply regretted his decision. 'You have built what you or others could have built anywhere,' he declared, 'but you have destroyed something that was unique in the world.' The damage could not be undone, and the cathedral now sits uneasily in the mosque.

A bridge has spanned the river here at Córdoba since Roman times.

Several gateways provide access through the high wall surrounding the Mezquita, the most impressive being the monumental Mudéjar **Puerta del Perdón** (Gate of Forgiveness). You pass through the ceremonial forecourt of the **Patio de los Naranjos** with its fountains and venerable orange trees, to reach the entrance to the mosque. Inside, as your eyes adjust to the dim light, you will see mesmerizing rows of columns extending into the shadows in every direction. Antique shafts of porphyry, onyx, marble and jasper, they seem to grow out of the paving stones like trees in an enchanted forest, a deliberate mirroring of the trunks of the orange trees in the courtyard outside. The double arches overhead, striped red and white, form a fanciful canopy of curving branches.

At the far end, set in the south-east wall, is the splendid 10th-century **mihrab**, lined with marble and gold mosaics, and the *maksourah*, the enclosure where the caliph attended to his prayers. In the central area of the mosque, restorers have exposed to view a section of the original carved and painted wooden ceiling, which had been covered over with vaulting in the 18th century.

The **cathedral** seems lost in the immensity of the mosque (it covers an area of 2 hectares/ 5 acres). But once you find it – at the very centre of the forest of pillars – the understated simplicity of Islamic design fades completely from view. Jasper and marble gleam down from the high altar, and mahogany lends lustre to the ornate choir stalls, a tour de force of baroque wood-carving.

On the very periphery of the cathedral, two Mudéjar chapels dating from the 14th century echo the ornament of the *mihrab* and *maksourah* – the **Capilla de Villaviciosa** and the not quite so resplendent **Capilla Real**.

Other chapels line the perimeter of the mosque. A few of them are being dismantled, but no one will touch the Capilla de San Bartolomé, where the great 16th-century poet, Luís de Góngora, lies buried.

A Selection of Hotels and Restaurants on the Costa del Sol

Recommended Hotels

The following hotels are listed alphabetically, covering Málaga and Marbella on the coast, and the cities of Sevilla, Córdoba and Granada inland. Telephone and fax numbers have been included for making direct bookings with the hotel. The Spanish hotel gradings (see ACCOMMODATION on p.108) are given in brackets after each name.

Prices do not normally include breakfast, so check before you book. As a basic guide we have used the symbols below to indicate the price for a double room with bath or shower in the high season. Low season rates can be considerably lower.

▯▯▯▯	over 15,000 ptas
▯▯▯	10,000-15,000 ptas
▯▯	5,000-10,000 ptas
▯	below 5,000 ptas

CÓRDOBA

González (H**) ▯▯
Manríquez 3, Córdoba
Tel. (957) 479819; fax 486187
Small, family-run hotel in a quiet back street near the Mezquita. Lovely Moorish decor, and pleasant flower-bedecked patio. No parking. 17 rooms.

Maimónides (HR***) ▯▯▯–▯▯▯▯
Torrijos 4, Córdoba
Tel. (957) 471500; fax 483803
Boasts a pretty Andalucian patio inside, and an ideal location next door to the tourist office, across the street from the Mezquita. Underground garage. 83 rooms.

Meliá Córdoba (H****) ▯▯▯▯
Jardines de la Victoria, Córdoba
Tel. (957) 298066; fax 298147
Luxury hotel set in lovely gardens in city centre, with views over the Mezquita to the river. 147 rooms.

El Oasis (H*) ▯▯
Avenida de Cádiz 78, Córdoba
Tel. (957) 298311; fax 291311
Comfortable hotel situated on edge of town, conveniently located on approach from Sevilla, but still only a few minutes' drive from the Mezquita. Swimming pool and car park. 50 rooms.

Parador de la Arruzafa (H****)

Avenida de la Arruzafa 33, Córdoba
Tel. (957) 275900; fax 280409
A modern *parador* on the edge of town, with all mod cons including pool and tennis courts. 94 rooms.

Hostal las Tendillas (HsR**)

Jésus María 1, Córdoba
Tel. (957) 473029
A pleasant, simple *hostal* on the Plaza de las Tendillas in the heart of the new town, ten minutes' from the Mezquita. 15 rooms.

GRANADA

Alhambra Palace (H****)

Peña Partida 2, Granada
Tel. (958) 221468; fax 226404
A modern Moorish-style palace next to the Alhambra, with stunning views across the city and up to the Sierra Nevada. 144 rooms.

Hotel América (H*)

Real de la Alhambra 53, Granada
Tel. (958) 227471; fax 227470
A pretty little hotel actually within the walls of the Alhambra citadel. Understandably popular, so book well in advance. Closed around November to February. 13 rooms.

Gran Vía Granada (H***)

Gran Vía de Colón 25, Granada
Tel. (958) 285464; fax 285591
Comfortable modern hotel conveniently located in the middle of the city's main thoroughfare. Underground garage. 85 rooms.

Los Jeronimos (H**)

Gran Capitán 1, Granada
Tel. (958) 294461; fax 294462
A pleasant, good value hotel in the university area of the city, about 20 minutes' walk from the Alhambra. Parking. 30 rooms.

Parador San Francisco (H****)

Real de la Alhambra, Granada
Tel. (958) 221440; fax 222264
A small and beautiful *parador* set within the precincts of the Alhambra, housed in the 15th-century convent where Queen Isabella was originally buried. The views from the bedrooms are magnificent. Book well ahead. 36 rooms.

Washington Irving (H***)

Paseo del Generalife 2, Granada
Tel. (958) 227550; fax 228840
Stylish, old-fashioned hotel in the wooded *alameda* beneath the Alhambra walls. Elegant wood-panelled bar. 68 rooms.

67

MÁLAGA

El Cenachero (P**)   ▐-▊▊
Barroso 5, Málaga
Tel. (95) 2224088
Bright and pleasant *hostal* in main accommodation district south of Alameda Principal. 14 rooms.

Málaga Palacio   ▊▊▊▊
(HR****)
Cortina del Muelle 1, Málaga
Tel. (95) 2215185; fax 2215186
Large city centre hotel set a block away from the cathedral and next to the lively and colourful streets of the old town, with rooftop swimming pool. 225 rooms.

Los Naranjos   ▊▊▊▊
(HR***)
Paseo de Sancha 35, Málaga
Tel. (95) 2224317; fax 2225 975
Modern six-storey hotel in a calm residential area at the east end of town, and only 1km from the beach. 41 rooms.

Parador Málaga-   ▊▊▊▊
Gibralfaro (H****)
Monte de Gibralfaro, Apdo de Correos 274,
Málaga
Tel. (95) 2221902; fax 2221904
A small *parador* beside the Moorish castle on the hilltop above the city. Grand views over the city and the bay. Reservations recommended. 36 rooms.

Sur (H**)   ▊▊
Trinidad Grund 13, Málaga
Tel. (95) 222 4803; fax 2212416
Adequate rooms, but convenient location in heart of restaurant- bar-nightclub district, just off Alameda, and only ten minutes' stroll from the cathedral. 37 rooms.

MARBELLA

Las Chapas (H***)   ▊▊▊
Carretera Cádiz Km 192
Tel. (95) 2831375; fax 2831377
Holiday complex set amongst pine trees beside the beach about 8km (5 miles) east of town. Watersports facilities. 117 rooms.

La Estrella (P**)   ▊▊
Calle San Cristóbal,
Marbella
Tel. (95) 2779472
Cheap, centrally located pension on edge of Old Town (signposted from main road). 15 rooms.

Guadalpin (H***)   ▊▊-▊▊▊
Carretera Cádiz Km 179
Tel. (95) 2771100; fax 773334
Functional modern hotel with very pleasant gardens, at western edge of town. Swimming pool. Parking. 103 rooms.

Hostal Guerra (Hs*)

*Llano San Ramón 2,
Marbella*
Tel. (95) 2774220
Clean, bright and friendly *hostal* a
few blocks east of the town centre,
five minutes' walk from the Old
Town. Excellent value. 6 rooms.

Los Monteros ||||+
(H*****GL)

Carretera Cádiz Km 188
Tel. (95) 22771700; fax 22823846
The Costa del Sol's most expensive
and luxurious hotel, complete with
an 18-hole golf course, 11 tennis
courts, five squash courts and a
riding club. 171 rooms.

Paco (P**)

Peral 16, Marbella
Tel. (95) 2771200
Picturesque hotel in back street in
the Casco Antiguo (Old Town), a
few minutes' stroll from the Plaza
de Naranjos (Square of the Orange
Trees). Closed around October to
March. 25 rooms.

Puente Romano ||||+
(H*****GL)

Carretera Cádiz Km 178
Tel. (95) 22770100; fax 22775766
Beautiful luxury hotel in Andalucian style, with a genuine Roman
bridge in the extensive landscaped
gardens. 184 rooms.

SEVILLA

Alfonso XIII ||||++
(H*****GL)

San Fernando 2, Sevilla
Tel. (95) 4222850; fax 216033
One of Spain's top hotels, the Alfonso XIII was built in 1929. The
sumptuous rooms are decorated
in Andalucian style, and the grand
lobby bar is a meeting point for
Sevilla's high society. 149 rooms.

Bécquer (H***) |||

Reyes Católicos 4, Sevilla
Tel. (95) 4228900; fax 4214400
Comfortable modern hotel near
the river, convenient for shops and
restaurants, approximately 20 minutes' walk from cathedral. Garage.
120 rooms.

Murillo (H**) ||

Lope de Rueda 7, Sevilla
Tel. (95) 4216095; fax 4219616
An atmospheric hotel hidden deep
in the heart of the historic Barrio
de Santa Cruz. 57 rooms.

Simón (H*) ||-|||

García de Vinuesa 19, Sevilla
Tel. (95) 4226660; fax 4562241
Fine, handsome hotel set in a renovated 18th-century town house
well-situated just across the street
from the cathedral. Attractive
patio. 31 rooms.

69

Recommended Restaurants

The establishments recommended here are mostly traditional Andalucian restaurants serving up local specialities. The resorts along the coast are packed with cheaper (and blander) alternatives, ranging from fast-food joints to Chinese, Indian, and Italian restaurants. Seafood restaurants line the waterfront in every town, and are usually expensive – head inland a block or two and the prices drop considerably, though the quality remains the same. Reservations are recommended for the more expensive places.

As a basic guide, we have used the following symbols to give some idea of the cost of dinner for two, excluding drinks.

▯▯▯	over 10,000 ptas
▯▯	6,000-10,000 ptas
▯	below 6,000 ptas

CÓRDOBA

El Churrasco ▯▯▯
Romero 16, Córdoba
Tel. (957) 290819
The city's best-known restaurant, specializing in fish and grilled meats prepared according to local recipes. Menu varies according to season. Closed August.

El Tablón ▯
Cardenal González 69, Córdoba
Tel. (957) 476061
Standard Spanish specialities at very reasonable prices, especially considering the convenient location just around the corner from the Mezquita.

COSTA DEL SOL

Antigua Casa Guardia ▯
Alameda Principal 18, Málaga
No telephone
Not a restaurant but one of the oldest and most traditional *tapas* bars in town. Enjoy small dishes of prawns, clams, mussels and meatballs washed down with wine from the barrel.

El Cabra ▯▯
Paseo Pedregal 17, Pedregalejo, Málaga
Tel. (95) 2291595
The best and most popular of the many seafood restaurants lining the waterfront here.

Casa Guaquin ▮▮

Carmen 37, La Carihuela,
Torremolinos
Tel. (95) 2384530

A block away from the promenade means lower prices in this fine seafood restaurant. A great place to sample the local speciality, *dorada a la sal y al horno* (roasted sea bass in salt). Closed Thursday.

Mar de Alborán ▮▮

Avenida de Alay 5
Benalmádena-Costa
Tel. (95) 2446427

Near the marina in Benalmádena, this Basque-Andalusian restaurant specializes in good fresh seafood. Closed Sunday evening and all day Monday..

La Meridiana ▮▮▮

Camino de la Cruz s/n
Marbella
Tel. (95) 2776190

One of the best restaurants on the Costa del Sol. Top quality international cuisine, impeccable service. Dinner only in summer.

Meson El Chinitas ▮

Moreno Monroy 4, Málaga
Tel. (95) 2210972

Attractive restaurant in the heart of the Old Town specialising in Andalucian and *malagueño* specialities.

El Mirlo Blanco ▮

Plaza de la Constitutión, Mijas
Tel. (95) 2485700

Enjoy romantic dining on the terrace, overlooking the pretty main square of the village. Traditional Basque specialities.

Romy ▮

Moncayo10/12, Edificio Perlilla
Fuengirola
Tel. (95) 2464131

Excellent value *zarzuela* (seafood stew), garlic prawns and tender grilled meats. Lively terrace in pedestrianized street behind waterfront. Closed Thursday.

La Rueda ▮▮

San Miguel 1, Benalmádena
Tel. (95) 2448221

A popular eating place with local residents. The menu includes international cuisine and local dishes like partridge in Málaga wine. Terrace dining in summer. Closed Tuesday.

Ventorrillo de la Perra ▮▮

Avenida de la Constitución 85
Arroyo de la Miel
Tel. (95) 2441966

What was once an old roadside inn now a restaurant serving an interesting mix of local, regional and international dishes. Closed Monday.

GRANADA

El Amir ▯▯
General Narváez 3, Granada
Tel. (958) 266818
If you want a change from Spanish food, try this North African restaurant – delicious *falafel*, *hummus*, *baba ganoush* and *couscous* amongst others, all washed down with refreshing mint tea.

Mirador de Morayma ▯▯
Pianista García Carrillo 2,
Albaicín, Granada
Tel. (958) 228290
This romantic Andalucian restaurant offers some fine views over the city. Closed Sunday evening.

Sevilla ▯▯
Oficios 12, Granada
Tel. (958) 221223
Granada's most famous restaurant, it was also once a favourite of García Lorca. The menu offers a good mixture of local Granadan and Andalucian specialities. Closed Sunday evening.

SEVILLA

La Albahaca ▯▯▯
Plaza Santa Cruz 12, Sevilla
Tel. (95) 4220714
A beautiful gourmet restaurant in the heart of the pretty Santa Cruz

district, with al fresco dining in summer. Closed Sunday.

Ox's ▯▯–▯▯▯
Betis 61, Sevilla
Tel. (95) 4279585
Another traditional restaurant offering Basque specialities. Closed Sunday evening, and August.

El Rinconcillo ▯
Gerona 42, Sevilla
No telephone
One of the oldest and most atmospheric *tapas* bars in the city, dating from the 17th century, and literally seething with *sevillana* high society. For a taste of true Sevilla.

Rio Grande ▯▯▯
Betis s/n, Sevilla
Tel. 4273956
Spectacular views across the city and the Guadalquivir river from the terrace and main dining area make this restaurant a must. Andalusian dishes are a speciality.

San Marco ▯▯▯
Cuna 6, Sevilla
Tel. 4212440
Quality restaurant set in a historic mansion in the heart of old Seville. The decor is stunning and the menu offers a range of inventive dishes from traditional Sevillian to Italian and nouvelle cuisine.

A Christian king, Alfonso XI, built Córdoba's **Alcázar de los Reyes Cristianos**, overlooking the river to the south west of the mosque. The ramparts offer a fine view over the old town and the river, the islets in mid-stream each occupied by a ruined Moorish mill, and the blue ridges of the Sierra de Córdoba low on the horizon. A great water wheel once irrigated the beautiful gardens of the Alcázar.

North of the mosque lies the labyrinth of narrow streets that make up the **Barrio de la Judería** (Jewish Quarter). Some of the best restaurants and *tapas* bars in Córdoba are to be found here. Sights to look for include the 14th-century synagogue (*sinagoga*) in the street called Judíos. It's a modest affair, just one small room, with a balcony for female worshippers. Córdoba's Jews helped the Moors to gain control of the city in 711, and they lived in peace under the caliphate.

Perhaps the most illustrious resident of the neighbourhood was Moses Maimonides. A statue of the 12th-century doctor, philosopher and theologian stands a few steps from the synagogue in the square named in his honour, **Plaza de Maimonides**. The little **Museo Municipal de Arte Cordobesa y Taurino** (Municipal Museum) on the square displays some examples of Córdoba craftsmanship (silver filigree, tooled leather), and mementoes of the bullfight.

North east of the mosque, the splendid Renaissance Palacio Paéz houses the **Museo Arqueológico Provincial**. The exhibits span the centuries from the Iberian era to the Visigothic period, but pride of place goes to objects from the 10th-century palace of Medina Azahara, like the bronze figure of a stag taken from a fountain presented by the Byzantine emperor Constantine VII.

Don't miss the 16th-century Palacio de los Marqueses de Viana, with its thirteen patios, and the Plaza de la Corredera, dating from the 17th century.

Ten kilometres (6 miles) north west of Córdoba lie the ruins of **Medina Azahara**, discovered in 1944 and now **73** partly restored. The summer palace of the Ummayad rulers was commissioned in 936 by Abd-er-Rahman III for his favourite wife, Zahara, only to be laid waste by Berber soldiers in 1010. The reconstructed royal apartments give some impression of the original magnificence of this sumptuous complex of baths, schools, gardens and stately apartments.

GRANADA

Granada was the last of the great Moorish cities of Andalucía to fall, and its surrender to Ferdinand and Isabella in January 1492 marked the end of the Muslim empire in Spain. Approaching Granada from Motril, you get your first view of the city as you cross over the pass called El Puerto del Suspiro del Moro – the Pass of the Sigh of the Moor – so named because Boabdil, the last Moorish king, paused here to take one last look at the city he had lost.

Boabdil was the last of the Nasrid dynasty, which rose to power in Granada just as the fortunes of the Spanish Moors were beginning to wane (see p.17). The first of the line, Mohammed ben Alhamar, established his capital here in 1232, after Ferdinand III had forced him from Jaén. Two years later, Moors fleeing from the newly vanquished Sevilla swelled the population, which had already been augmented by refugees from Córdoba. Rather than grieve for the homes they had left behind, the industrious Moors set about making Granada the grandest city of Al Andalus. Over the course of the next century, the hilltop palace of the Alhambra took shape.

The **Alhambra** (The Red) takes its name from the red-brown bricks used in the construction of its outer walls, which rise precipitously above the deep gorge of the Río Darro. Its towers command superb views over the white-walled, red-roofed houses of the old Albaicín quarter, and across to the Sacromonte caves, where Granada's gypsy community lives in homes tunnelled out of the soft rock. To approach the Alhambra on foot, climb

GRANADA

steeply up the Cuesta de Gomerez from the Plaza Nueva. This narrow street lined with souvenir shops and *hostales* leads through a triple-arched gateway into the green-dappled shade of the **Alameda**, a leafy glade beneath the fortress walls. (The gate is topped with three pomegranates, the city's emblem – *granada* is Spanish for pomegranate. However, the city's name is more probably a corruption of the Moorish name, *Karnattah*, the Hill of Strangers.) A steep pathway on the left leads to a wall fountain, above and behind which lies the Puerta de la Justicia, a gate tower with three bends inside to obstruct invading troops.

Within the walls of the Alhambra, there are three main areas to explore, best taken in the following order: the Alcazaba, or fortress; the Palacio Nazaries, or Royal Palace; and finally the Generalife, or summer gardens. The increasing number of tourists has led to the introduction of a special ticket system which allots a specified half-hour time slot during which you must enter

the Palacio Nazaries. You can stay as long as you like once you're in, but you must enter during the period stated on your ticket. Allow an hour or so for the Alcazaba beforehand. (Visitors on organized tours need not worry, as tickets will have been arranged for them.)

Of the **Alcazaba**, the oldest part of the Alhambra, only the outer walls and towers survive, but these are sufficiently impressive. The main attraction is the view from the Torre de la Vela, north over Albaicín and Sacromonte, and south to the high snow-capped peaks of the Sierra Nevada.

The highlight of your visit will undoubtedly be the **Palacio Nazaries** (Palace of the Nasrids), the magnificent home of the rulers of the kingdom of Granada. Entering through the **Mexuar** (council chamber) and the small courtyard that adjoins it, you pass into the strik-

Intricate decoration testifies to the art, skill and patience of Moorish craftsmen.

ing **Patio de los Arrayanes** (Court of the Myrtle Trees), where Moorish colonnades, clipped hedges, a reflecting pool full of fish, and tinkling fountains make for a perfect Arabian Nights setting. The adjacent **Salón de Embajadores** (Hall of the Ambassadors), or royal audience chamber, is

one of the most sumptuously ornamented rooms in the Alhambra. Skirted with geometric tiling, the walls and roof are overlaid with delicately shaped plaster stalactites, reaching 18m (60ft) to the carved and painted wooden ceiling. Verses from the Koran and the name of the 14th-century monarch Yusuf I are woven into the design. Tall, horseshoe-arch windows frame views of Albaicín and the Darro so magnificent that Charles V was moved to remark, 'Ill-fated was the man who lost all this'.

A gallery at the far end of the Patio de los Arrayanes communicates with the enchanting **Patio de los Leones**. The name of this square derives from the plashing fountain in the centre, upheld by 12 stone lions, symbols of strength and courage. A graceful colonnade surrounds the fountain on four sides, its slender columns and tent-roofed pavilions creating an atmosphere of sunlit contemplation, and splendid rooms flank the courtyard on every side. The **Sala de Abencerrajes** (with its elaborate stalactite

ceiling) recalls the aristocratic family of that name, who were accused of disloyalty and collusion with the Christians by Boabdil, the last king of Granada (see p.74). The king invited the Abencerrajes to a reception in this very room, and massacred all (unsuspecting) 36 family members.

Paintings of Moorish and Christian kings decorate the ceiling of the **Sala de los Reyes** (Hall of the Kings). The subject is unusual in a Moorish palace – Islam proscribes the representation of images of humans and animals – but the Nasrid kings were far more influenced by Christian customs than the teachings of the prophet Mohammed.

In the **Sala de las Dos Hermanas** (Hall of the Two Sisters), an exquisite latticework shutter, the only surviving example in the whole palace, covers the gracefully arched window opposite the entrance. A honeycomb-patterned cupola rises overhead, the walls below decorated with an overlay of silvery-blue stucco, incised with the greatest delicacy. A pair of identical white marble slabs set in the floor on either side of the fountain are the 'two sisters' that give the room its name.

The lavishly decorated **Mirador de Lindaraja**, once the the queen's bedroom, juts out above a peaceful courtyard planted with cypress and fragrant orange trees. On the opposite side of the courtyard lie the **Apartments of Charles V**, a suite of rooms used by the Christian emperor, who shunned the Moorish arabesques for the sober charms of an Italianate fireplace embellished with dolphins. This is where the novelist Washington Irving

American writer Washington Irving recorded Moorish folk tales in Tales of the Alhambra.

Washington Irving

Irving was an American writer from New York, who is best known for *The Sketch Book*, a collection of stories which included such classics as *The Legend of Sleepy Hollow* and *Rip Van Winkle*. From 1826 until 1832 he was attached to the American legation in Spain, where he became fascinated by the legends of Moorish Andalucía. During his stay in Granada he moved into the apartments of Charles V while writing *Tales of the Alhambra*, a collection of romantic stories about Granada's Moorish past. It is on sale all over town, and is well worth reading.

took up residence while composing his *Tales of the Alhambra* in 1829.

Overlooking the grand Palacio Nazaries is the **Palacio de Carlos V** (Palace of Charles V), a structure that has been much maligned for its intrusive character – and for the fact that a section of the earlier Moorish palace was razed to make way for it. But considered on its own merits, the building must be regarded as a fine example of Renaissance architecture.

Pedro Machuca, a student of Michelangelo, designed the palace in 1526; bullfights were once staged in its circular courtyard. The emperor, ever short of funds, financed the construction work with a tax levied on the *moriscos* (see p.18). Work on the building came to an abrupt halt when the *moriscos* eventually revolted, and the palace remains unfinished to this day.

Two museums are housed inside the palace. The **Museo Nacional de Arte Hispano-Musulmàn** (Museum of Hispano-Moorish Art) displays such evocative artefacts as the throne of the Nasrids, a wooden armchair inlaid with silver and ivory, and the tombstone of 15th-century king, Muley Hassan. His love for a Christian girl precipitated a civil war that put his son, Boabdil, on the throne and eventually led to the fall of the kingdom. The highlight of the museum's exquisite collection is the Alhambra Vase, which once graced the Hall of the Two Sisters; it is the finest surviving example of 15th-century Spanish-Moresque ceramics.

The **Museo de Bellas Artes** (Fine Arts Museum) is a largely uninspiring collection of religious works chronicling the development of the school of Granada between the 16th and 19th centuries.

At the eastern end of the Alhambra fortifications, a footbridge leads to the terraced gardens of the **Generalife** (pronounced khay-nay-rah-*lee*-feh, from the Arabic *Jennat al-Arif*, the Garden of the Architect) on the neighbouring hillside. The modest summer palace is surrounded by beautiful gardens, where oleander and roses bloom luxuriantly, and delicate fountains and cascades play among the neatly clipped cypress hedges. The Generalife's terraces afford lovely views of the Alhambra and Albaicín.

Granada's vast cathedral is an imposing structure, towering above the east end of the Gran Via, but the exquisite **Capilla Real** (Royal Chapel) at its side steals its thunder. The great masterpiece of Enrique de Egas, this Renaissance chapel serves as the mausoleum of the Catholic Monarchs. The façade, with its twisted columns and blind arcade, displays remarkable dignity and refinement, qualities that apply equally to the interior, with its splendid wrought-iron grilles and marble funerary monuments. The effigies of Ferdinand and Isabella lie on the right-hand side of the chancel, with those of their daughter

Beautiful gardens complement the architectural treasures of the Alhambra.

Juana La Loca (Joan the Mad) and her husband Felipe El Hermoso (Philip the Fair) on the slightly higher monument on the left. Their mortal remains lie in the crypt below, contained in simple caskets of lead.

Exhibited in the **sacristy** are Ferdinand's sword and Isabella's sceptre and crown, a circle of gold embellished with acanthus scrolls. On the walls hang superb 15th-century works of

art from queen Isabella's personal collection, including Rogier Van der Weyden's moving *Pietà*, an emblematic *Head of Christ* by 15th-century Dutch painter Dierick Bouts, and Botticelli's *Christ in the Garden*.

A few steps from the chapel, the **Alcaicería**, the old silk market of the Moors, has been revived as a centre for handicrafts and souvenirs, but for

*M*arble effigies of Spanish monarchs recline in Granada's Capilla Real.

a more genuine taste of old Granada, wander the narrow streets and staircases in the old Moorish district of **Albaicín**, with its ancient white houses, enclosed patio gardens, and stunning views across the Darro to the Alhambra.

The gypsies of the Sacromonte may try to tempt you to an impromptu flamenco show in one of their cave houses – one of the world's best-known tourist traps: be warned! Don't accept their offers unless, of course, you want to be cleverly parted from every last peseta in your possession.

What to Do

Sports

Although many visitors to the Costa del Sol will not be planning any activity more energetic than unscrewing the top of the Ambre Solaire bottle, sports facilities are there in abundance for those who want to work off the effects of too much *paella* and San Miguel. Watersports, golf, tennis, hiking – take your pick.

WATERSPORTS

The main resort beaches offer all kinds of sports equipment for hire, as well as beach umbrellas and loungers. The larger beach restaurants (*merenderos*) have toilet facilities, and some provide changing rooms.

Swimming: with more than 160km (100 miles) of beaches to choose from, the Costa del Sol offers plenty of scope for swimming. Most of the sandy strands lie to the west of Málaga, while sandy coves, shingle

and rock largely predominate to the east, where the mountains plunge steeply down to the sea. In the high season, the main beaches are mobbed – you stand the best chance of finding a patch of sand to yourself to the east of Nerja and west of Estepona.

Like all other resorts in the Mediterranean, the Costa del Sol has had to deal with the problem of polluted waters and dirty beaches. Legislation has been introduced to discourage ships from dumping oil off the coast, and a sophisticated sewage treatment system has gone into operation, greatly improving the quality of the water. Special beach-grooming vehicles patrol the more popular beaches in the early morning, cleaning up rubbish, seaweed and other debris.

Boating: there are ten marinas along the coast between Málaga and Sotogrande, providing year-round moorings for yachts and motor boats and, in some cases, making hire and charter arrangements. Marbella alone boasts three harbours: Puerto **83**

Banús, Puerto Deportivo and Puerto Cabopino. In addition, most of the tourist beaches and larger beach hotels have small sailboats for hire – Hobie Cats, Toppers, Wayfarers, and some may offer instruction.

Water-skiing: the main resorts all have water-ski schools, and most big hotels also offer instruction. Prices are generally high, but they do vary. You can save money if you shop around and most schools give some kind of discount for multiple runs paid in advance.

Try to go out early in the morning, when seas are calm and there are fewer swimmers about. Swimming and skiing areas often overlap as the day goes by, so don't automatically expect a clear run if you are a power boat driver or a skier – even if you're in the reserved ski area. There is in fact a new cable-ski park near San Pedro de Alcántara.

Windsurfing: this sport is the coast's fastest-growing activity, with boards, sails and professional tuition available in

Carving a turn at San Pedro de Alcántara's cable-ski park couldn't be more thrilling.

most of the resort areas. The season runs from March to November, though winds are generally at their strongest in June and September.

Snorkelling and Scuba Diving: snorkelling can be an engrossing activity, particularly off the rocky, indented stretch of coast beyond Nerja. If you swim any distance from the shore, you are legally required to tow a marker buoy. Diving centres operate in several resorts, and in Gibraltar. They provide boats and equipment, and, in some cases, tuition, and can also arrange for the necessary diving permits. For more information, contact the Spanish National Tourist Office (see p.128).

Angling: fishing from the rocks and breakwaters is a popular pastime with the locals – no permit is required. The deeper waters offshore teem with tunny (tuna), swordfish and shark. Deep-sea fishing boats can be hired at the marinas, and many resort hotels make arrangements for fishing expeditions.

A very popular inland fishing spot is the Pantanos del Chorro ('pantano' meaning 'reservoir'), at the Chorro Dam (see p.31). Freshwater anglers must have a permit – ask at the nearest tourist office for information on how to obtain one.

OTHER SPORTS

Golf: when it comes to variety of courses, few resort areas in the world can compare with the Costa del Sol. There are nearly thirty 18-hole courses between Málaga and Gibraltar. Most private and hotel clubs welcome non-residents or non-members, though some may charge visitors a slightly higher fee. Clubs, caddies, trolleys and electric carts are generally available for hire.

The quality of the courses is excellent – many have been designed by such famous names as Robert Trent Jones and Seve Ballesteros. Las Brisas, near Marbella, has hosted the Spanish Open, and has been the venue for two World Cups. Also in the Marbella **85**

*L*ocals as well as tourists relax or pursue their chosen activity on the river or down by the sea.

area is La Dama de Noche, a floodlit nine-hole course for those golf addicts who want to play after the sun goes down.

For details of golf courses and fees, consult the monthly magazine *Costa Golf*, an English-language publication, or the booklet 'Golfing in Spain', issued by the Spanish National Tourist Organization.

Tennis and Squash: Some of the biggest names in tennis are linked to the numerous clubs, centres and 'ranches' on the

Costa del Sol, including the Marbella-based Manolo Santana Tennis Club, which hosts the majority of Spain's Davis Cup matches and other important tournaments. Consult the local press for up-to-date details of events. Most of the big hotels have their own courts; for information about public courts, ask at the local tourist office.

Hiking: there are a number of good hiking areas within easy reach of the coast, notably the Montes de Málaga National Park just north of Málaga, and El Torcal and El Chorro a little further inland (see p.31). For more good walks, try the area around Ronda, and in the hills above the Refúgio de Juanar near Marbella (see p.41).

Hunting: the foothills of the sierras harbour rabbit and partridge, while deeper in the mountains lurk deer and wild goat, including the elusive ibex (see p.41). There are good hunting grounds in the area north of Marbella, especially in the Serranía de Ronda and, closer to the coast, the Sierra Blanca (see p.41). The season for game runs roughly from the months of September to December, while small animals may generally be hunted from October to February. A hunting permit is required. Enquire at the tourist office for more information.

Horse riding: Andalucía is famous for both its horses and horsemanship. There are numerous stables on the coast, with mounts for hire; you can canter along the open beach or ride up into the hills. Twelve-day horseback tours of Andalucía are organized from Arcos de la Frontera. Inquire at the tourist office for details.

Skiing: few people think of the Costa del Sol as a skiing resort, but nevertheless, skiing can be enjoyed between December and May at the Solynieve resort near Granada, 160km (100 miles) north east of Málaga in the Sierra Nevada. Situated near the summit of Mount Veleta, it is Europe's most southerly ski resort.

Shopping

Real estate may be the fastest selling item on the Costa del Sol, but if you're not in the market for a holiday flat or timeshare villa, there are plenty of other things to look for. Traditional Spanish handicrafts are high on any souvenir-hunter's shopping list – ceramics, basketry and wrought-iron work, not forgetting rugs.

Leather goods, while no longer the bargain they once were, compare favourably in price with Italian- and French-made articles, and the local factories do turn out stylish, high-quality leather clothing. Córdoba, which has been producing leather goods since Roman times, is famous for its embossed leather.

Weekly open-air markets are held Mondays in Marbella, Tuesdays in Nerja and Fuengirola, Wednesdays in Estepona, Thursdays in Torremolinos and San Pedro de Alcántara and Fridays in Benalmádena. Fuengirola and Estepona also have a Sunday market.

Where to Shop

The city of Málaga offers lower prices and a better selection of goods than resorts like Torremolinos or Fuengirola. You'll want to browse along the main

The streets of Mijas are lined with interesting craft shops and souvenir stalls.

Siesta

The *siesta* is an afternoon nap taken to avoid the hottest part of the day. What it means for the visitor is that many shops and businesses take a three-hour lunch break, closing from 1 or 2pm to 4 or 5pm, then opening up again until 7.30pm. This age-old custom seems to be dying out in some parts of northern Spain, but it is still observed in Andalucía.

shopping thoroughfares in the old town – Calle de Larios, Calle de Granada (a continuation of Larios) and Molina Lario, and pay a visit to the huge Corte Inglés department store.

For more sophisticated shopping, nothing can compare with Marbella or nearby (and luxurious) Puerto Banús, where dozens of attractive, harbourfront boutiques offer a stunning selection of merchandise – at a price, of course.

You can make a considerable saving on luxury goods like jewellery, watches, perfumes and Havana cigars in duty-free Gibraltar, where the dreaded VAT does not exist, but make sure you don't exceed your allowance or you will have to cough up the tax at customs when you return home.

Opening Hours

Most establishments are open from 9.30 or 10am to 1.30 or 2pm and from 4.30 to 8pm. The siesta (see above) is still religiously observed in southern Spain. In summer, shops in the tourist resorts keep longer hours, staying open all day until 8.30pm or sometimes later. Department stores do not close for the siesta.

Tax Rebates for Visitors

The Spanish government levies a value-added tax (called IVA) on most items (currently at 7 percent). Tourists from outside the EU will be refunded the IVA they pay on purchases over a stipulated amount. To obtain the rebate, you have to **89**

*B*ric-a-brac abounds in the tourist resorts, but genuine antiques are rare.

fill out a form, which the shop will provide on request. The shop keeps one copy; the three others must be presented at customs on departure, together with the goods, and the rebate is then forwarded by the shop to your home address. It can prove worthwhile if spending **90** a lot in one place.

Best Buys

Basketwork: alongside goods made in Hong Kong and the Philippines, you'll see authentic Andalucian articles – sturdy shopping baskets, wine carriers, sombreros – even saddle-bags of plaited straw.

Brassware: look for hand-beaten bowls and pitchers in traditional forms.

Ceramics: the everyday, functional, glazed terracotta pottery produced in Almuñécar and other towns can be bought all along the coast. There's also a wide selection of tiles (*azulejos*), vases, bowls and jugs, with floral or geometric decorations.

Foodstuffs: take home a taste of Spain with some olives, olive oil, almonds, and *membrillo* or quince paste.

Jewellery: silver rings, bracelets and necklaces in modern designs make good buys, as do the artificial 'Majorica' pearls of Spain. Look, too, for fine filigree jewellery from Córdoba, and smooth, polished olivewood beads.

Leather and suede: choose from a wide selection of locally made handbags, belts and wallets, and attractive trousers, skirts, jackets and coats.

Records, cassettes, CDs: the range of Spanish recordings includes *zarzuela* tunes and flamenco music, and classical works by Rodrigo, Albeniz, Granados and De Falla.

Rugs: durable and colourful Granada-style woollen rugs are cheaper in Granada than down on the coast. Some shops along the coast – particularly in the village of Mijas – will make rugs to order.

Souvenirs: often delightfully tacky, from plastic castanets and flamenco dolls, to imitation wine skins and even bullfight posters printed with your own name.

Wine and spirits: sweet Málaga wine, sherry, brandy, and

At the market, you can stock up with fresh herbs and spices as well as souvenirs.

Spanish wines provide some of the best bargains in Spain (see p.104), and even good labels are much more affordable than back home.

Wooden articles: salad bowls, pepper mills and nutcrackers of olive wood make appealing gifts and souvenirs. **91**

Entertainment

Organized Outings

Tour operators offer lake swimming and boating excursions and farmhouse barbecue parties (flamenco entertainment is optional). *Burro* safaris, long a feature of Costa del Sol tourism, involve an hour's ride from a mountain village to a *paella* party out of doors. Make bookings through your hotel or a local travel agent.

Amusement Parks

The Atlantis Aquapark in Torremolinos, open daily from 10am to sundown, boasts a kamikaze water slide billed as Europe's highest, and a wave pool that generates 2m (6ft) breakers. Beach areas, waterfalls, whirlpools and a restaurant all contrive to pull in the crowds. Fuengirola's equivalent is the smaller Mijas Aquapark, right beside the N-340, open daily 10am to 5.30pm.

Like its rather more illustrious namesake in Copenhagen,

Tívoli World (in Arroyo de la Miel, between Torremolinos and Fuengirola) offers nightclubs, restaurants and bars, in addition to flamenco shows and all the thrills and spills of fairground rides and attractions. Open Easter to October, 6pm to midnight.

Bullfights

The bullfight is considered to be something between an art and a sport: look in a Spanish newspaper and you will see that the bullfight is reported in its own section between these two categories.

The Costa del Sol has some good rings – notably at Málaga, Estepona and Marbella – but apart from Málaga, the bullfights on the coast are for the most second string events, where the *novilleros* (novice bullfighters) learn their trade. The top performers can be seen in Sevilla and Córdoba, where the spectators are at their most demanding. Fights are held once a week in Seville during the season, which lasts from March to October. Most

CALENDAR OF EVENTS

January: *Cabalgata de Reyes* (Three Kings Parade). Málaga. On the eve of Epiphany (5 January), floats, bands and traditionally costumed characters commemorate the visit of the Wise Men to the infant Christ.

March/April: *Semana Santa* (Holy Week). Throughout the area. Sombre processions of hooded penitents and religious images take place nightly during the week before Easter. Most impressive in Sevilla, where accommodation becomes thin on ground and, to a lesser extent, in Málaga.

April: *Feria de Abril* (April Fair). Sevilla. Horses and riders, bullfights and flamenco, and parties in the streets are part of Andalucía's most colourful festival.

April/May: *Feria del Caballo* (Horse Fair). Jerez de la Frontera. Spain's equestrian showcase, with events of all kinds, including racing, dressage and carriage competitions.

May: *Romería de San Isidro* (Pilgrimage of St Isidore). Estepona, Nerja. Decorated carts and costumed riders parade in Estepona, while Nerja stages concerts, folk dancing and fireworks.

June: *Corpus Christi*. Throughout the area. Bullfights and fireworks enliven this national holiday, a big event in Granada.

June/July: *Festival Internacional de Música y Danza*. Granada. Concerts and dance performed out of doors in the Alhambra and Generalife.

July: *Virgen del Carmen*. Coastal towns. Processions of fishing boats pay tribute to the Virgin of Carmen, protectress of fishermen.

August: *Feria de Málaga* (Málaga Fair). A funfair, circus, bullfights and flamenco events enliven the first fortnight of the month in Malaga. *Festival de España*. Nerja. The town's famous cave provides the eery venue for this subterranean celebration of music and dance.

September: *Feria de Ronda* (Ronda Fair). The highlight of this fair is the *corrida goyesca*, a costumed bullfight held in Ronda's 18th-century ring. *Fiesta de la Vendímia* (Wine Harvest Festival). Jerez de la Frontera. A parade, bullfights, flamenco and horse events follow the blessing of the harvest.

major centres hold regular bullfights during this period, and smaller towns often stage fights daily during town fairs and religious festivals. You may be enthralled – or appalled – by the spectacle, but whatever your reaction you'll gain a valuable insight into the country and the people.

For another perspective on the *fiesta brava*, watch a televized fight, complete with action replays and close-ups.

The Bullfight

This 'ballet of death' is a ritualized encounter between man and bull. In a typical *corrida*, three matadors take on two bulls each – menacing animals, three to five years old.

Each fight comprises three acts, or *tercios*. The first begins with the release of the bull into the arena. Members of the *cuadrilla*, followed by the matador himself, begin to control the animal with their wide magenta capes. Then the *picadores* enter the ring, mounted on horses girdled in protective padding. They attack the bull's neck with their lances, weakening its neck muscles so that its head will stay low for the kill.

The second act brings on the *banderilleros*, who run obliquely across the path of the charging bull, and attempt to plunge pairs of beribboned steel darts (*banderillas*) into the bull's shoulders.

In the final *tercio*, the 'act of death', known as *'la suerte de la muerte'*, the matador takes centre stage to confront the bull alone. He plays the bull with his small red cape or *muleta*, drawing the angry beast close to his body and passing it neatly by him. When he has judged that the right moment has arrived, the matador moves in for the kill. Facing the bull head on; sword poised in front of him, he rises on his toes and leans forward over the horns to thrust the blade deep between the bull's shoulder blades. If the matador is judged to have performed exceptionally, he may be awarded one or both of the bull's ears. And very occasionally, if the bull has displayed extraordinary courage and stamina, it may be allowed to live.

Flamenco

Flamenco shows for tourists are laid on in all the coastal resorts. These shows can be entertaining, but the performances are more show business than the true spirit of flamenco. To experience flamenco at its most authentic, you will have to search out bars and small clubs in Málaga or Sevilla, where impromptu performances take place – ask the local tourist office for advice on where to go. Touring dance companies often take part in the summer festivals organized in many towns. Look in the local press for announcements of special events.

Flamenco is an ancient art form, combining elements of Visigothic, Moorish and gypsy music. There are two distinct types – the *cante jondo* (deep song), an intense outpouring of emotion, and the animated *cante chico* (light song). There are also different varieties of flamenco dance – the *tango*, *fandango*, *farruca* and *zambra* – performed to the staccato rhythms and counter-rhythms

*F*iery flamenco dancing is one of the traditional art forms of southern Spain.

of the castanets, hand-clapping (*palmadas*) and finger-snapping (*pitos*), as well as furious heel-drumming (*zapateado*). Flamenco dancing is high in colours and terribly dramatic: no need to speak Spanish to enjoy the spectacle. In fact, all Andalucians maintain that **95** flamenco can be understood, though not explained. There's nothing deep about the music – you simply have to feel it.

Discotheques and Nightclubs

Some discos open as early as 9pm, but most places don't gear up for business until 11pm or midnight. They close late, too, around 4 or 5 in the morning. Nightclubs (*salas de fiesta*) usually stage two shows an evening, one at about midnight or 1am and the other around 3am. Depending on the club, the show may feature flamenco performances, drag acts or girlie shows. Bars, pubs and clubs often provide musical entertainment in the form of a band or a singer, and a few also have a regular stand-up comic.

Casinos

Two gambling establishments operate from 8pm to 4am – the Casino Torrequebrada in Benalmádena-Costa (on the old N-340), and the Casino Nueva Andalucía in Puerto Banús's Hotel Nueva Andalucía, also on the coastal highway. In addition to the usual games available – American and French roulette, blackjack, *chemin de fer* and other 'classics' – the casinos have a bar, restaurant and nightclub on the premises. Formal dress is required in all establishments, and don't forget to bring your passport along for identification.

Concerts

From May to October, Tívoli World brings the stars of rock and pop to Torremolinos for concerts in the open air. The season's programme may include occasional performances of flamenco and *zarzuela* (Spanish light opera).

Year-round town fairs and celebrations will often include popular concerts, but – fans be warned – there's little in the way of classical music during the summer season. In winter, Málaga's symphony orchestra performs in the Teatro Cervantes theatre, and guest artists appear at Castillo El Bil-Bil in Benalmádena-Costa.

Cinema

There are cinemas in most towns, but the films are nearly always dubbed into Spanish. Films are sometimes screened in the original version at film clubs in Málaga – but this is certainly the exception rather than the rule.

Children on the Costa del Sol

The Spanish love children, and are very tolerant of their behaviour in restaurants and other public places. So don't be afraid to take yours along when you go out for a meal – it's what the locals always do.

The Costa del Sol is an ideal holiday location for families with kids – it's one long beach. Apart from paddling and sand castles, older children can learn how to sail, water-ski or wind-surf (see p.85). If you don't feel happy about letting your children play in the sea, especially the younger ones, the aquaparks at Torremolinos and Fuengirola offer a safer and more controlled environment where it's easier to keep a close eye on them. There are also exciting water slides and wave pools to play in, which should keep most children entertained for a good few hours.

Alternative diversions for children include the Sea Life aquarium in Puerto Marina (see p.34), the zoo in Fuengirola (see p.35), the Cueva (cave) de Nerja (see p.49), and Mini Hollywood near Almería (see p.52) In the evenings, Tívoli World, near Benalmádena (see p.34), provides all the fun of the fair, with fairground rides and a roller coaster, and there's also a bar and flamenco show for the grown-ups.

And when you're on the beach, don't forget that kids are especially vulnerable to the effects of too much sun. Take along plenty of high-factor sunscreen, and a sun-hat each, and make sure they're covered up during the middle of the day (a siesta during the hottest part of the day may be a good idea). Nothing is more certain to spoil a holiday than sun-burnt offspring.

Eating Out

You could easily spend your entire holiday on the Costa del Sol without ever sitting down to a Spanish meal. In the big coastal resorts the range of eating places is amazing – hamburger stands, pizza bars, pub grub, beach barbecues and restaurants of almost any nationality you can think of, from Indonesian to Arabic, German to Japanese, Swedish, Dutch, French, Chinese, Indian – just about everything, except Spanish. In fact, you could dine on bacon and eggs, beans on toast, and steak and chips every day, without going into the same restaurant twice. For those visitors adventurous enough to want to sample the local fare, however, here is a quick guide to what to expect.

WHERE TO EAT

One of Spain's most civilized institutions is the **tapas bar**, or **tasca**, where you can order small helpings of tasty morsels to nibble on as you enjoy your drink – a fine way of sampling a lot of different dishes without filling your stomach or emptying your wallet.

Next step up the gastronomic ladder is the **comedor**, or dining room, often a small area at the back of a bar where you

Enjoy a cool drink beneath the shade in one of Marbella's sidewalk cafés.

can sit down and tuck into a basic but satisfying meal. *Comedors* tend, on the whole, to cater to local workers: cheap and cheerful, they are usually open for lunch only.

Cafeterias are middle-range eateries, common on the seafront in the resorts, and usually offer a selection of *platos combinados* (combination dishes), such as pork chop and chips, or calamares and salad, with bread and a drink included. The menu often consists simply of photographs of the various dishes.

Restaurantes proper are pretty much the same as back home; they are usually only open for lunch and dinner, and close one day a week. They may offer a *menú del día* (set menu), which will be cheaper than ordering à la carte.

A restaurant calling itself a **marisquería** specializes in seafood, while an **asador** is the place for roast meats. A **venta** is a small, family-run restaurant serving good down-to-earth country fare, and well worth looking out for if you venture away from the coast.

First-time visitors to Spain are often surprised by the late eating hours – Spaniards rarely sit down to lunch (*almuerzo*) before 2pm, and dinner (*cena*) starts around 10pm. However, most restaurants begin serving an hour or two earlier, and you do get quicker service if you arrive early. In the resort areas, many restaurants stay open all through the day. Although service is included in the bill, it is customary to leave an additional tip (see p.128).

WHAT TO EAT

Breakfast

The traditional Spanish breakfast is not for the faint-hearted, and generally consists of *churros y chocolate* (doughnut-like fritters and thick, sweet drinking chocolate) taken standing up at the counter in a downtown café. Alternatively, try a *tostada con aceite* (toasted roll with olive oil) washed down with *café con leche* (milky coffee). Spanish expresso (*café solo*) is strong stuff, even with a touch of milk (*un cortado*). **99**

*S*eafront restaurants tempt passers-by with displays of al fresco cookery.

Hotels may offer a more substantial affair – fruit juice, cereal, eggs, sausages, toast and so on. In the tourist resorts, several cafés offer traditional British breakfasts.

Tapas

Every good bar offers a selection of *tapas*, bite-size morsels to accompany your drinks. The name comes from the practice, now almost vanished, of providing a free titbit with every drink. The food was served on **100** a small plate traditionally used

to cover the glass, and came to be called a *tapa*, which literally means 'lid'.

Among the dozens of items to choose from you may find sweet red peppers in olive oil seasoned with garlic, Russian salad, slices of sausage – both spicy *chorizo* and paprika-flavoured *salchichón* – or *jamón serrano* (cured ham), marinated mussels, baby squid, clams, *tortilla española* (Spanish omelette, with potato and onion filling, usually served cold in slices). For a larger serving of any given tapa, ask for a *ración*. If you feel that's too much for you, order a *media-ración*.

Vegetable Dishes

Spaniards usually eat vegetables as a first course, rather than as an accompanying dish. But whatever you do, don't miss that great speciality of Andalucía, *alcachofas a la Montilla* – tender artichoke leaves cooked in a mixture of wine and beef broth, thickened with flour and seasoned with mint, garlic and saffron. *Judías verdes con salsa de tomate*, green beans in tomato sauce, laced with garlic, can be very good. Other popular greens include *guisantes* (peas), *lentejas* (lentils), *espinacas* (spinach) and *habas* (broad beans).

Soups

Andalucía's most famous speciality is the cold soup known as *gazpacho*. There are dozens of ways to make it, but the version you are likely to find in southern Spain is a creamy, chilled blend of cucumber, tomato, onion and crushed garlic, with freshly-diced green pepper, tomato and cucumber, chopped hard-boiled egg, and fried croutons on the side.

Originally from Málaga, *ajo blanco* (white garlic soup) is a variation on the more common gazpacho theme. Ground almonds and garlic form the base of this summer refresher,

served ice-cold with a garnish of almonds and grapes.

Be sure to try the mixed fish or shellfish soups, *sopa de pescado* and *sopa de mariscos*. Like its French counterpart, the Mediterranean bouillabaisse, *sopa marinera* is based on the day's catch, and seasoned with tomato, onion, garlic and a dash of white wine or brandy.

Egg Dishes

Egg dishes make popular starters, and a whole Spanish omelette is a filling lunch on its own. *Tortillas* (omelettes) may be filled with asparagus, tuna or mushrooms. *Huevos a la flamenca* is a baked dish of eggs cooked on a base of tomato, garlic and herbs – usually accompanied with diced ham or spicy *chorizo*, fresh peas and sweet red peppers.

Paella

Spain's most famous dish deserves to be discussed separately. The main ingredient is saffron-flavoured rice, cooked in a large frying pan with olive **101**

The name paella comes from the flat, round metal pan it is cooked in; aficionados claim that simmering over an open fire is the best way to prepare this hearty dish.

Seafood

Fish and shellfish are understandably popular, and invariably fresh. The seafood you are served in the waterfront restaurants was landed on the beach that very morning by the fishermen whose boats lie hauled up on the sand.

The traditional Torremolinos lunch is sardines skewered on a wooden spike and grilled over a charcoal fire on the beach. This simple but tasty dish is quite simply irresistible and extremely good value.

For more adventurous diners, squid may be an interesting option, either cooked in

oil, seafood and chicken. But every chef has his own personal variation on this colourful dish that originated in Valencia, on Spain's eastern coast. The secret of perfect paella is fresh ingredients – fresh seafood such as *langosta* (spiny lobster), *langostinos* (a kind of large shrimp), *cigalas* (giant prawns or sea crayfish), *gambas* (prawns), mussels, and chicken, peas, sweet peppers and artichoke hearts, all cooked together slowly as the rice absorbs the juices.

its own ink (*calamares en su tinta*), a spicy dish, or simply dipped in batter and fried, and served with a twist of lemon. *Gambas* and *cigalas* are large juicy prawns – choose your own from the display and have them grilled while you choose your wine. When it's available, the *langosta* (lobster) is excellent served hot with butter, or cold with mayonnaise, though you should be warned that it never comes cheap.

Boquerones (fresh anchovies) and *chanquetes* (whitebait) are tossed in flour and deep fried whole. *Merluza*, or hake, may be served fried, boiled, or mushroom-stuffed, perhaps with tomatoes and potatoes. *Besugo* (sea bream) is a high-quality fish, brushed with olive oil and simply grilled.

Other common items on the menu may include *pez espada* (swordfish), *mero* (sea bass), *bonito* (tuna) and *rape* (monkfish). If you have difficulty deciding what to try, you may want to plump for the *fritura malagueña*, a mixed fish fry that includes all of the above seafood and more.

Chicken and Meat

If you have forgotten the flavour and aroma of real chicken, as opposed to the tasteless, battery-farmed, frozen supermarket fowl back home, then you're in for a treat. Spanish chicken is delicious, whether fried, roast, or braised in white wine or sherry with almonds. The staple *arroz con pollo* (chicken with rice) is tasty too.

Many traditional Andalucian meat dishes make use of offal such as tripe, brains and sweetbreads. If these make you feel squeamish, then opt for something a little more mainstream like *riñones al Jerez*, kidneys sautéed with sherry, or *rabo de toro*, braised oxtail served in a rich tomato sauce with carrots and spices. *Ternera a la Sevillana*, veal in a sherry sauce with green olives, is a speciality of Sevilla. Rabbit (*conejo*) or hare (*liebre*) in white wine forms the basis of many a tasty casserole.

Steak and various cuts of beef are available – although not quite on a par with what's served in the Argentine or in **103**

Texas. A local variation on this international standard is *bistec a la mantequilla de anchoas* (beefsteak with an anchovy-butter sauce).

Cheese and Dessert

Spaniards eat cheese (*queso*) after the main course, notably the tangy *queso de manchego* – fresh, smoked or in oil – and the milder *queso de Burgos*, widely available on the coast. You may also come across *queso de cabrales*, a combination cheese made from goat's, cow's and sheep's milk in the north-western province of Asturias. After ageing it becomes blue-veined, and has a sharp taste rather simalar to Roquefort. *Idiázabal* is a smoked and cured goat's cheese.

Fruits in season include *uvas* (grapes), *higos* (figs), *melón* (melon), *naranjas* (oranges), *melocotón* (peach), *chirimoyas* (custard apples), *fresas* (strawberries) and *cerezas* (cherries).

Besides ice cream, southern Spain offers pastries and cream desserts in abundance. One appealing preparation is *brazo de gitano*, a rolled sponge cake with rum-flavoured cream filling. The obiquitous *Flan*, or egg custard with caramel sauce, invariably appears on menus all over Spain. Eggs cooked with sugar make a thickened custard called *natillas*.

WINE AND SPIRITS

Wine is produced all over the country, but the most famous is Rioja from the Ebro valley in the north-east. The white wines of Rioja, dry or sweet, are considered quite drinkable, but Rioja reds are the glory of Spain – the aged Gran Reservas (at least five years old) are comparable to some of France's noblest red wines, though Riojas have a character all of their own, and do not necessarily resemble Bordeaux or Burgundies. Labels to look out for include Marqués de Riscal, Siglo, CUNE, Berberana and Campo Viejo.

Navarre, north of the Ebro valley, also produces some interesting red wines (look for Campanas, Señorío de Sarría, Murchante). From La Mancha, between Madrid and Andalucía, come Valdepenas wines, which are both light, crisp and pleasing to the palate – a staple for sangria. Reds and whites from Catalonia will also appear on Costa del Sol wine lists. Labels to look for include Torres and Rene Barbier. Many restaurants have their own inexpensive table wine – *vino de la casa* – which can prove an acceptable alternative.

Spain also boasts a mass-produced sparkling wine of the champagne type, referred to as *cava*, which may be rather on the sweet side for northern palates. Among the best are Gran Cordorniu or Cordorniu Non Plus Ultra.

Sangria needs little introduction – this iced combination of red wine and brandy with lemon, orange and apple slices, makes a great refresher for beach or balcony at any time of day. It packs a punch, however, so you might want to mix in some soda water.

An aristocrat among wines, *jerez* (sherry) is grown in the chalky vineyards around Jerez de la Frontera. It is aged according to centuries-old tradition in long rows of casks or butts, by blending the young wine with a transfusion of mature sherry – a method known as *solera*.

Fino, the driest of sherries, is a light, golden aperitif which should be served chilled. A type of fino, called *manzanilla*, is slightly richer; Sanlúcar de Barrameda *manzanilla* is especially good. *Amontillado*, usually medium dry, is a deeper gold in colour, and is heavier than a true fino. *Amoroso* is medium sweet, with an amber colour, and *oloroso* is still more full-bodied. As for cream sherries, they are sweet and more deeply coloured.

The Andalucía region produces several other semi-sweet to sweet wines, most notably the sweet, mahogany-coloured wine of Málaga, called *Málaga dulce* (rather like port), and the wines of Montilla-Moriles, near Córdoba.

Spanish brandy, or *coñac*, tends to be heavy, but it is usually drinkable and reasonably priced. The more expensive brands are much smoother. **105**

To Help You Order ...

Could we have a table?		¿Nos puede dar una mesa?	
Do you have a set menu?		¿Tiene un menú del día?	
I'd like a/an/some ...		Quisiera ...	
beer	**una cerveza**	milk	**leche**
bread	**pan**	mineral water	**agua mineral**
coffee	**un café**	napkin	**una servilleta**
cutlery	**los cubiertos**	potatoes	**patatas**
dessert	**un postre**	rice	**arroz**
fish	**pescado**	salad	**una ensalada**
fruit	**fruta**	sandwich	**un bocadillo**
glass	**un vaso**	sugar	**azúcar**
ice cream	**un helado**	tea	**un té**
meat	**carne**	(iced) water	**agua (fresca)**
menu	**la carta**	wine	**vino**

... and Read the Menu

aceitunas	olives	**judías**	beans
albóndigas	meatballs	**lenguado**	sole
almejas	baby clams	**mariscos**	shellfish
atún	tunny (tuna)	**mejillones**	mussels
bacalao	cod	**ostras**	oysters
besugo	sea bream	**pastel**	cake
calamares	squid	**pimiento**	sweet red pepper
callos	tripe		
cangrejo	crab	**pulpitos**	baby octopus
cerdo	pork	**salchichón**	salami
champiñones	mushrooms	**salmonete**	red mullet
chuletas	chops	**salsa**	sauce
cordero	lamb	**ternera**	veal
entremeses	hors-d'œuvres	**trucha**	trout
106 **huevos**	eggs	**uvas**	grapes

BLUEPRINT
for a
Perfect Trip

An A–Z Summary of Practical Information

Listed after some entries is the appropriate Spanish translation, usually in the singular, plus a number of phrases that should help you when seeking assistance.

A

ACCOMMODATION (*hotel; alojamiento*)
(See also CAMPING on p.110, YOUTH HOSTELS on p.132 and the list of RECOMMENDED HOTELS AND RESTAURANTS starting on p.66)
Package holidays tend to provide accommodation in hotel complexes and self-catering apartments, while those travelling independently will find a wide range of options. If you plan to visit during the high season you should book accommodation well in advance, through a travel agent or directly with the hotel. The Spanish National Tourist Office (see TOURIST INFORMATION OFFICES on p.128) provides a comprehensive annual listing of all graded hotels (including room rates).

By law, prices must be displayed in reception and in the rooms. Meals (including breakfast) are not usually included in the basic rate, and VAT (IVA in Spanish) of 7 percent (15 percent in five-star hotels) will be added to your bill.

Establishments are graded according to the following system, with one of the following ratings plus the number of stars:

Hotel (H): rated one to five stars according to services offered. The most expensive option, topped only by **Hotel Grand Luxe (HGL)**, signifying absolute top-of-the-range accommodation.

108 Hotel Residencia (HR): same as a hotel, but there is no restaurant.

Hostal (Hs): a more modest hotel, often a family concern, graded one to three stars. Rates overlap with the lower range of hotels, e.g. a three-star *hostal* usually costs about the same as a two-star hotel.

Hostal Residencia (HsR): as for a *hostal*, but without a restaurant.

Pensión (P): a boarding house, graded one to three stars, with only basic amenities.

Fonda (F): a village inn, fairly inexpensive, clean and unpretentious.

Casa de Huéspedes (CH): a guesthouse. Bottom of the scale, but usually clean and comfortable as well as cheap.

Casa Rural: country house offering bed-and-breakfast or self-catering accommodation.

Parador: a state-run hotel, often housed in a castle or other historic building. Of special interest to motorists, since they are usually located on the outskirts of towns. Advance booking essential.

In addition, each town offers countless cheap ungraded rooms to let – look for signs reading '*camas*' (beds) or '*habitaciones*' (rooms).

I'd like a single/double room with bath/shower	**Quisiera una habitación sencilla/doble con baño/ducha**
What's the rate per night?	**¿Cuál es el precio por noche?**

AIRPORTS (*aeropuerto*)

The Costa del Sol is served by Málaga's **Aeropuerto Internacional**, situated some 8km (5 miles) west of the centre of Málaga, and 7km (4½ miles) from Torremolinos. There is a bus service every 30 minutes to Málaga, Torremolinos and Benalmádena-Costa, as well as a half-hourly train service (follow the signs marked '*ferrocarril*') to central Málaga and the coastal resorts from Torremolinos to Fuengirola. Taxis can be found at the taxi rank outside the terminal. The journey from the airport to central Málaga or Torremolinos takes about 10 to 15 minutes, and about 20 minutes to Fuengirola.

Where's the bus for…?	**¿De dónde sale el autobús para…?**

B

BICYCLE and MOPED HIRE
(*bicicletas/velomotores de alquiler*)

Bicycles can be hired in Torremolinos, Fuengirola and Marbella on a daily or weekly basis. Rates for mopeds are considerably higher. Insurance is obligatory and costs extra, and a deposit will also be required. A special motorbike licence is needed for machines of over 50cc, and the wearing of crash helmets is compulsory.

I'd like to hire a bicycle.	**Quisiera alquilar una bicicleta.**
What's the charge per day/week?	**¿Cuánto cobran por día/semana?**

C

CAMPING (*camping*)

There are numerous official campsites (*campings*) along the Costa del Sol and throughout Andalucía, including those at Torremolinos, Fuengirola, Mijas, Marbella and Estepona. Facilities vary, but most sites have electricity and running water, many have shops and children's playgrounds, and some even have launderettes and restaurants. Rates depend to a large extent on the facilities available. For a complete list of campsites, consult the *Guía de Campings*, available from local bookshops, or from the Spanish National Tourist Office (see TOURIST INFORMATION OFFICES on p.128).

Camping outside of official sites is permitted, provided you obtain permission from the landowner. However, you are not allowed to pitch your tent on tourist beaches, in urban areas, or within 1km of an official site.

110 May we camp here?   **¿Podemos acampar aquí?**

CAR HIRE (*coches de alquiler*) (See also DRIVING, p.116)

There are numerous car-hire firms in the tourist resorts and main towns; local firms often charge considerably less than the big international chains. Rates vary enormously, and you should shop around for the lowest price. The best rates are usually to be had by booking and paying for your car before you leave home, either directly through the office of an international rental company at home, or as part of a 'fly-drive' package deal. Check that the quoted rate includes Collision Damage Waiver, unlimited mileage and VAT (IVA in Spain), as these can increase the cost considerably. Theft from cars is rampant on the Costa del Sol, and theft insurance is an extra worth considering. Extra cover against theft of radio and other car parts, and damage caused by thieves is very reasonable and worth considering.

Normally you must be over 21 to hire a car, and you will need a full, valid driver's licence (EU model) which you have held for at least 12 months, your passport, and a major credit card – cash deposits are prohibitively large.

I'd like to hire a car (tomorrow).	**Quisiera alquilar un coche (para mañana).**
for one day/a week	**por un día/una semana**
Please include full insurance.	**Haga el favor de incluir el seguro a todo riesgo.**

CLIMATE and CLOTHING

Plenty of hot sunshine and cloudless skies – that's the rule, not the exception on the Costa del Sol. There are, nevertheless, seasonal variations worth noting when you choose your holiday time. From June to September, hot days with low humidity are followed by slightly cooler evenings; rain is a rarity. In April, May and October daytime temperatures remain quite warm, but it can get cold at night. From November to March, shirt-sleeve sunshine can still be enjoyed, but may be interrupted by chill winds from the mountains and even rain – on average four to six rainy days a month in winter. Overleaf, you will find the average monthly temperatures for Málaga.

	J	F	M	A	M	J	J	A	S	O	N	D
max.°C	16	17	18	20	23	25	28	29	26	23	19	17
min. °C	10	11	12	13	15	18	20	21	19	17	14	11
max.°F	60	62	65	68	73	78	83	83	79	73	66	62
min. °F	50	51	54	56	60	64	68	69	67	62	57	53
sea °C	15	14	15	16	17	21	21	23	21	18	17	14
°F	59	57	59	60	62	69	69	73	69	65	62	57

Clothing. From June to September the days are always hot – wear lightweight cotton clothes – but take along a jacket or sweater for the evenings. Remember also to take a long-sleeved shirt and sunhat to protect against the strong midday sunshine. During the rest of the year a light jacket and a raincoat or umbrella will come in handy.

Respectable clothing should, of course, be worn when visiting churches – long trousers or skirt and long-sleeved shirt or blouse – but women are no longer expected to cover their heads.

COMMUNICATIONS (See also TIME DIFFERENCES on p.127)

POST OFFICES (*correos*)

Post offices handle mail and telegrams only; normally you cannot make telephone calls from them. Hours vary slightly from town to town, but routine postal business is generally transacted from 8.30am to 2.30pm, Monday to Friday, 9.30am to 1pm only on Saturday. There is generally only one post office per town, and it is usually very busy. Fortunately, postage stamps (*sellos*) are also on sale at tobacconists' (*estancos*) and hotel desks, and at tourist shops selling postcards. Mail for destinations outside Spain should be posted in the box marked *extranjero* (overseas).

Poste restante (general delivery). If you don't know ahead of time where you'll be staying, you can have your mail addressed to you c/o poste restante (*Lista de Correos*) in whichever town is most convenient, eg: Mr John Smith, Lista de Correos, Torremolinos, Spain. When collecting your mail, take your passport as identification.

Telegrams. Telegrams can be sent from post offices, or dictated by telephone (tel. 2222000 in Málaga), but they are expensive; if you do not know the Spanish, ask your hotel receptionist to do it for you. Night letters or night-rate telegrams (*telegrama de noche*) are delivered the following morning and cost much less than standard-rate messages.

Where is the (nearest) post office?	**¿Dónde está la oficina de correos (más cercana)?**
Have you received any mail for…?	**¿Ha recibido correo para…?**
A stamp for this letter/postcard, please.	**Por favor, un sello para esta carta/tarjeta.**
express (general delivery)	**urgente**
airmail	**vía aérea**
registered	**certificado**
I want to send a telegram to…	**Quisiera mandar un telegrama a…**

TELEPHONES (*teléfono*)

In addition to the telephone office in Málaga there are phone booths everywhere from which you can make local and international calls. Instructions in English and area codes for different countries are displayed in the booths. You'll need a supply of 5, 25 and 100 ptas coins – local calls cost around 15-25 ptas, calls to the UK are around 300-350 ptas a minute. Some telephones accept credit cards, and others use a phonecard (*tarjeta telefónica*), available from *tabacos*. For international direct dialling, pick up the receiver, wait for the dial tone, then dial 07, wait for a second tone and dial the country code, area code (minus the initial zero) and number. Alternatively, to make a reverse charge or British Telecom Chargecard call to the UK, dial 900 99 00 44 – this will put you straight through to a British operator.

Can you get me this number?	**¿Puede comunicarme con este número?**

COMPLAINTS

By law, all hotels and restaurants must keep official complaints forms (*hoja de reclamaciones*) and produce one on demand. The original of this triplicate document should be sent to the regional tourist authority, one copy remains with the establishment, and you keep the third sheet. Merely asking for a complaint form is usually enough to resolve any problems, since tourism authorities take a serious view of complaints and your host wants to keep both his reputation and his licence intact. If you fail to obtain satisfaction from the manager, take your complaint to the local tourist office (see TOURIST INFORMATION OFFICES, p.128).

CRIME

Spain's crime rate has increased dramatically in recent years, especially in the cities and some of the larger resorts. Muggings and petty theft are all too common these days, so it's only sensible to take certain precautions. Most crimes against tourists are non-violent, mainly bag-snatching, pickpocketing and theft from cars. If you are unfortunate enough to be attacked, don't offer resistance – some thieves are armed with knives. Always carry a minimum of cash, and keep your passport, traveller's cheques, credit cards and cash in a money belt or, better still, entrust your valuables to hotel safe-deposit boxes. Dress modestly and forswear jewellery – especially gold chains. Lock your car and stow any possessions out of sight in the boot (trunk), but *never* leave anything in your car overnight.

Certain areas and events frequented by tourists are a target for thieves – the footpath up to Gibralfaro in Málaga, for example, and the April *feria* in Sevilla. Inquire locally before you set out alone, especially at night. Don't be put off, however – remember that the great majority of prudent visitors enjoy a happy and carefree holiday.

All thefts must be reported to the police within 24 hours– you will need a copy of the police report in order to make a claim on your holiday insurance. If your passport has been stolen or lost, your consulate should also be informed (see p.119).

114 I want to report a theft.   **Ha habido un robo.**

CUSTOMS (aduana) and ENTRY FORMALITIES

For citizens of EU countries, a valid passport or identity card is all that is needed to enter Spain for up to 90 days. Other nationalities require a valid passport; Australian, Canadian and New Zealand citizens need a visa, obtainable from any Spanish embassy or consulate. British tourists must now have a full passport to enter Spain – a Visitors' Passport is no longer accepted. For stays of more than 90 days a special visa or residence permit is required. Full information on passport and visa regulations is available from the Spanish Embassy in your country (see EMBASSIES AND CONSULATES on p.119).

As Spain is part of the EU, free exchange of non-duty free goods for personal use is permitted between **Spain** and the **UK** and the **Republic of Ireland**. Duty-free items are still subject to restrictions. Residents of non-EU countries can take home the following amounts: **Australia**: 250 cigarettes or 250g tobacco; 1l of wine or 1l of spirits. **Canada**: 200 cigarettes and 50 cigars and 400g of tobacco; 1.1l of wine or 1.1l of spirits or 8.5l of beer. **New Zealand**: 200 cigarettes or 50 cigars or 250g tobacco; 4.5l of wine or beer and 1.1l of spirits. **South Africa**: 400 cigarettes and 50 cigars and 250g tobacco; 2l of wine and 1l of spirits. **USA**: 200 cigarettes and 100 cigars and a reasonable amount of tobacco; 1l of wine or 1l of spirits.

Currency restrictions. Tourists may bring an unlimited amount of Spanish or foreign currency into the country. On departure you must declare any amount beyond the equivalent of 1,000,000 pesetas.

It's for my personal use.   **Es para mi uso personal.**

D

DISABLED TRAVELLERS

Facilities for the disabled are improving all the time, but as yet public transport is not wheelchair accessible. The Spanish National Tourist Office (see p.128) provides a useful fact sheet and a list of accessible accommodation.

The Spanish national organization for the **blind** is ONCE (Organización Nacional de Ciegos de España), tel. (91) 431 1900.

DRIVING

Motorists planning to take their vehicle abroad need a full driver's licence, an International Motor Insurance Certificate, and a Vehicle Registration Document. A green card is not a legal requirement, but is strongly recommended for travel within Spain. A nationality plate must be displayed near the rear number plate, and headlamp beams must be adjusted for driving on the right. You are also advised to carry a bail bond. (If you injure somebody in an accident in Spain, you can be imprisoned while the accident is under investigation. This bond will bail you out.) Full details are available from your Automobile Association, or from your insurance company.

The use of seat belts (front and back seats) is *obligatory.* A red warning triangle must be carried. Motorcycle riders and their passengers must wear crash helmets.

Driving conditions. Drive on the right, overtake (pass) on the left. Give way to traffic coming from the right. Speed limits are 50kph (30mph) in built-up areas, 90-100kph (55-60mph) on highways, and 120kph (75mph) on motorways. Note that Spanish drivers tend to sound their horn or flash their headlights when overtaking.

Main roads and motorways are generally very good and improving all the time; secondary roads less so. New bypasses around Málaga and the coastal resorts of Torremolinos, Benalmádena, Fuengirola, Marbella and Estepona have vastly improved road conditions on the N-340. The stretch of road between Motril and Almería is still narrow and twisting and plagued with slow-moving lorries.

Parking (*aparcamiento*). Parking regulations are strictly enforced – offending vehicles will be towed away (*grua*), and a hefty fine charged for their return. A yellow-painted kerb means parking is prohibited at all times, blue means parking is restricted to certain times – check the signs (a Spanish dictionary is useful!).

Traffic police. Spanish roads are patrolled by the motorcycle police of the Civil Guard (*Guardia Civil*). They are efficient with minor mechanical problems and go out of their way to help you if you have a breakdown. They can impose on-the-spot fines of up to 50,000 ptas on offending motorists. The most common offences include speeding, overtaking without flashing your lights, travelling too close to the car in front, and driving with burned-out lights. (Spanish law requires you to carry a set of spare bulbs at all times.)

Fuel and oil. Service stations are plentiful, but it's a good idea to keep an eye on the gauge in the more remote areas like the Alpujarra.

Breakdowns. Spanish garages are as efficient as any, but in tourist areas major repairs may take several days because of heavy workload. Spare parts are readily available for all major makes of cars.

Road signs. Most of the road signs used in Spain are international pictograms. But here are some written signs you will come across:

Aduana	Customs
¡Alto!	Halt!
Autopista (de peaje)	(Toll) motorway (expressway)
Calzada deteriorada	Bad road
Calzada estrecha	Narrow road
Ceda el paso	Give way (Yield)
Circunvalación	Bypass/ring-road
Cruce peligroso	Dangerous crossroads
Cuidado	Caution
Curva peligrosa	Dangerous bend
Despacio	Slow
Desviación	Diversion (Detour)
Escuela	School
Obras	Road works (Men working)
¡Pare!	Stop!
Peligro	Danger

Prohibido adelantar	No overtaking (passing)
Prohibido aparcar	No parking
Puesto de socorro	First-aid post
Salida de camiones	Lorry (Truck) exit
Sin plomo	Unleaded petrol
(International) Driving Licence	**carné de conducir (internacional)**
car registration papers	**permiso de circulación**
green card	**carta verde**
Can I park here?	**¿Se puede aparcar aquí?**
Full tank, please, top grade.	**Llénelo, por favor, con super.**
Check the oil/tyres/battery.	**Por favor, controle el aceite/ los neumáticos/la batería.**
There's been an accident.	**Ha habido un accidente.**

Entering Gibraltar. You must be in possession of a green card to visit Gibraltar by car, which means that tourists driving hired cars may not cross the border. They can, however, park on the Spanish side, cross on foot and take a taxi on the other side (see p.43).

Distance

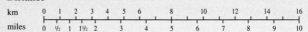

Fluid measures

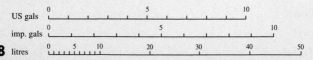

ELECTRIC CURRENT (*corriente eléctrica*)

220V/50Hz AC (*doscientos veinte*) is now standard, but older instal-
lations of 125 volts (*ciento veinticinco*) can still be found. Check! An
adaptor for continental-style two-pin sockets will be needed; American 110V appliances will also require a transformer.

an adaptor/a battery   **un adaptador/una pila**

EMBASSIES and CONSULATES (*embajadas y consulados*)

Australia: Federico Rubio 14, 41004 Sevilla, tel. (95) 4220240.

Canada: Edificio Horizonte, Calle Cervantes, Málaga, tel. (95)
2223346; Avenida de la Constitución 30, Sevilla, tel. (95) 4229413.

Republic of Ireland: Avenida de los Boliches 15, Fuengirola,
tel. (95) 2475108.

UK: Edificio Duquesa, Calle Duquesa de Parcent 8, Málaga,
tel. (95) 2217571; Plaza Nueva 8, Sevilla, tel. (95) 4228875.

US: Centro Comercial Las Rampas II, Fuengirola, tel. (95) 2474891.

EMERGENCIES (*emergencias*)

Unless you are fluent in Spanish you should seek help through your
hotel receptionist or the local tourist office. If you can speak Spanish,
the following telephone numbers may be useful.

	Fire	Ambulance	Police
Fuengirola	2461046	2303034	091
Málaga	080	2303034	091
Marbella	2774349	2303034	091
Torremolinos	2383939	2303034	2389999

GUIDES and TOURS

An English-speaking guide can be hired through the local tourist office (see TOURIST INFORMATION OFFICES, on p.128), or by contacting the guide agency at Edificio Salomé, Carretera de Benalmádena 4, Torremolinos; tel. (95) 2386042/5. Guided tours and excursions to Gibraltar, Ronda, Sevilla, Córdoba, Granada and other places can be booked through any of the numerous travel agencies (*agencia de viaje*) to be found in the coastal resorts.

LANGUAGE

The national language of Spain, Castilian Spanish, is spoken throughout the Costa del Sol area. Even if you learned Spanish at school, you might find the local accent a little difficult to understand at first. However, English is widely spoken in the resort towns, though it is polite to learn at least a few basic phrases. The Berlitz SPANISH PHRASEBOOK AND DICTIONARY covers most situations you are likely to encounter, and the Berlitz Spanish-English/English-Spanish pocket dictionary contains some 12,500 entries, plus a menu-reader supplement. For further useful expressions, see the cover of this guide.

LAUNDRY and DRY-CLEANING

Most hotels will handle laundry and dry-cleaning, but they'll usually charge a lot more than the local laundry (*lavandería*) or dry-cleaners (*tintorería*). For still greater savings, you can try a coin-operated launderette (*lavandería automática*), though these are thin on the ground outside the more popular resorts.

When will it be ready? **¿Cuándo estará lista?**

I must have this for **La necesito para mañana**
tomorrow morning. **por la mañana.**

LOST PROPERTY (*objetos perdidos*) (See also CRIME on p.114)

Ask for advice from your hotel receptionist or the local Tourist Information Office before contacting the police. For items left behind on public transport, ask your hotel receptionist to telephone the bus or train station or taxi company.

I've lost my wallet/ handbag/passport. **He perdido mi cartera/ bolso/pasaporte.**

MEDIA

Radio and Television (*radio; televisión*). Several local radio stations have broadcasts in English. Radio broadcasts can also be picked up from Gibraltar, and night reception is usually good enough to hear most European countries on medium-wave transistor portables, including the BBC World Service and the Voice of America. Network television programmes are all in Spanish. Better hotels also have satellite TV with CNN, MTV, Superchannel, Sky TV etc.

Newspapers and magazines (*periódico, revista*). In the major tourist areas you can buy most European newspapers on the day of publication, but at about three times the price. British and American magazines are also available. The weekly *Sur in English*, available free, is aimed at residents on the Costa del Sol and carries local news and events.

MEDICAL CARE

British and Irish citizens are entitled to free emergency hospital treatment – you should obtain form E111 from a post office before you leave in order to qualify. You may have to pay part of the price of treatment or medicines; keep receipts so that you can claim a refund when you return home. (Full details can be obtained from the Department of Health.) However, anything other than basic emergency treatment can be very expensive, and you should not leave **121** home without adequate insurance, preferably including cover for an emergency flight home in the event of serious injury or illness.

The main health hazard on the Costa del Sol is also its biggest attraction – the sun. Take along a sunhat, sunglasses, and plenty of high-factor sun-screen, and limit your sunbathing sessions to an hour or less until you begin to tan.

For minor ailments, visit the local first-aid post (*ambulatorio*). Away from your hotel, don't hesitate to ask the police or a tourist information office for help. At your hotel, ask the staff for assistance. *Farmacias* (chemist/drugstore) are usually open during normal shopping hours. After hours, at least one per town remains open all night, called *farmacia de guardia*, and its location is posted in the window of all other *farmacias*.

Where's the nearest (all-night) chemist?	**¿Dónde está la farmacia (de guardia) más cercana?**
I need a doctor/dentist.	**Necesito un médico/dentista.**
sunburn/sunstroke	**quemadura del sol/una insolación**
an upset stomach	**molestias de estómago**

MONEY MATTERS

Currency (*moneda*). The unit of currency in Spain is the *peseta* (abbreviated *ptas*). Coins in current circulation come in denominations of 1, 5, 10, 25, 50, 100, 200 and 500 pesetas, banknotes in 1,000, 2,000, 5,000, and 10,000 pesetas. A 5 ptas coin is traditionally called a *duro*, so if someone should quote a price as 10 duros, he means 50 pesetas. (For currency restrictions, see CUSTOMS AND ENTRY FORMALITIES on p.115.)

Banks and currency exchange offices (*banco, casa de cambio*). Banking hours are from 9am to 2pm Monday to Friday, and 9am to 1pm on Saturdays (winter only), closed on Sundays and public holidays. Outside normal banking hours, many travel agencies and *casas de cambio* (exchange offices) will change foreign currency and traveller's cheques into pesetas, though the exchange rate is less favourable than in the banks. Both banks and exchange offices pay slightly more for traveller's cheques than for cash, but there will be a fairly hefty commission, often a minimum of 500 pesetas per transaction. Always take your passport with you when you go to exchange money.

Traveller's cheques and credit cards (*cheque de viaje, tarjeta de crédito*). In the main towns and tourist areas, all banks, hotels and travel agencies and many shops accept traveller's cheques, though you're likely to get a better exchange rate at a national or regional bank. Cash only small amounts at a time, and keep your remaining cheques in the hotel safe if possible. At the very least, be sure to keep your receipt and a list of the serial numbers of the cheques in a separate place to facilitate a refund in case of loss or theft. All the major credit cards are accepted by hotels, restaurants, car-hire firms and other businesses. If you have a PIN, you can also use your credit card to obtain pesetas from Spanish cashpoint machines.

VAT (*IVA*). Remember that IVA (*impuesto sobre el valor agregado*), the Spanish equivalent of value added tax, will be added to your hotel and restaurant bills; it currently stands at 7 percent. A higher rate of 16 percent applies to five-star hotels and car hire charges and a rate of 4 percent applies to certain basic necessities.

PLANNING YOUR BUDGET

To give you an idea of what to expect, here's a list of some average prices in Spanish pesetas. They can only be approximate, however, as prices vary from place to place, and inflation in Spain, as elsewhere, creeps up relentlessly. Prices quoted may be subject to IVA of 4, 7 or 16 percent.

Bicycle and moped rental: Motorbike 4,000 ptas/day. Moped or scooter 2,500 ptas/day. Mountain bike 1,600 ptas/day.

Bus: Málaga to Fuengirola 280 ptas. Fuengirola to Gibraltar 1,550 ptas return trip.

Camping: 1st class: 2,000-3,000 ptas/day for a tent or caravan (trailer) or mobile home, plus 400-650 ptas/day per person. 3rd class: 350-500 ptas/day for a tent or caravan, plus 200-300 ptas/day per person. Reductions for children.

Car rental: *Ford Fiesta 1.1* 22,000 ptas/week, unlimited km, booked in Spain through a local firm; **or**, if booked in advance through a travel agent in the UK, around £100/week unlimited km, including collision damage waiver, personal accident insurance and tax.

Entertainment: Cinema from 450 ptas, flamenco nightclub (entry and first drink) from 2,500 ptas, discotheque from 1,000 ptas. Aquatic Park (per day) 1,550 ptas adult, 1,000 ptas child, 4,000 ptas family.

Hotels (double room with bath): ***** from 15,000 ptas, **** from 10,000 ptas, *** from 7,000 ptas, ** from 5,000 ptas, * from 2,800 ptas. Add 7 percent VAT, 16 percent in five-star hotels.

Meals and drinks: Continental breakfast 350-500 ptas, *plato del día* from 750 ptas, lunch/dinner in good restaurant from 3,000 ptas/head including wine, beer (small bottle or glass) 100-150 ptas, coffee 100-150 ptas, Spanish brandy 200-300 ptas, soft drinks from 150 ptas.

Shopping bag: Loaf of bread 70-200 ptas, 125g (4.5oz) of butter 180 ptas, dozen eggs from 200 ptas, 1kg (2.2lb) of steak 1,600 ptas, 250g (8oz) of coffee 325 ptas, 100g (4oz) of instant coffee 450 ptas, 2l (4 pints) of mineral water 100 ptas, bottle of wine from 280 ptas.

Sightseeing: Sevilla – Cathedral 550 ptas, Alcázar 600 ptas. Córdoba – Mezquita 600 ptas. Granada – Alhambra 600 ptas, Capilla Real 225 ptas.

Sports: Golf (per day) green fee 4,000–8000 ptas, caddie 2,500 ptas. Tennis court fee 1,000 ptas/hour, instruction from 3,000 ptas/hour. Windsurfing from 1,500 ptas/hour. Water-skiing 3,000 ptas/15 minutes. Jet ski 4,000 ptas/15 minutes. Parascending 4,000 ptas/flight. Horseback riding 2,000 ptas/hour.

Taxi: Average city centre trip 400–500ptas (rates vary from city to city). Long distances negotiable.

Train: Return ticket Fuengirola–Málaga 440 ptas weekdays, and 660ptas weekends and holidays.

I want to change some pounds/dollars.	**Quiero cambiar libras/dólares.**
Do you accept traveller's cheques?	**¿Acepta usted cheques de viaje?**
Can I pay with this credit card?	**¿Puedo pagar con esta tarjeta de crédito?**

OPENING HOURS

Banks are generally open 9am to 2pm Monday to Friday and 9am to 1pm on Saturday (winter only), closed Sunday and public holidays.

Post offices are open 8.30am–2.30pm Monday to Friday, 9.30am–1pm on Saturday, closed Sunday and public holidays.

Shops and offices and other businesses generally observe the afternoon siesta, opening 9.30am to 1.30pm, and 4.30 to 7.30pm, but in tourist areas many places now stay open all day.

SIGHTSEEING

Córdoba. The Mezquita opens daily 10am to 1.30pm and 4 to 7pm in summer, 10am to 1.30pm and 3.30 to 5.30pm in winter.

Gibraltar. The Apes' Den, Moorish Castle and Upper Galleries are open daily 10am to 7pm in summer, to 5pm in winter.

Granada. The Alhambra is open 9am to 8pm in summer, 9.30am to 5.45pm in winter. It is also open for floodlit tours from 10pm to midnight on Tuesday, Thursday and Saturday in summer.

Sevilla. The Alcázar opens from 10.30am to 5.30pm Tuesday to Saturday and 10am–1pm Sunday; La Giralda 11am to 5pm Monday to Friday, 11am–4pm Saturday and 2–4pm Sunday.

PHOTOGRAPHY (*fotografía*)

Major brands of film are widely available, but more expensive than in the UK, so stock up before you leave. Photo shops in major resorts can process your colour prints in 24 to 48 hours at reasonable prices, and some provide a one-hour service. The use of flash or tripod is forbidden in some museums and cathedrals.

I'd like some film for this camera.	**Quisiera un carrete para esta máquina.**
black and white film/ film for colour prints/ colour-slide film	**carrete en blanco y negro/ carrete para película en color/ carrete de diapositivas**
How long will it take to develop (and print) this?	**¿Cuánto tardará en revelar (y sacar copias de) este carrete?**

POLICE (*policía*)

There are three separate police forces in Spain – the *Policía Municipal*, who are attached to the local town hall and usually wear a blue uniform, are the ones to report theft and other crimes to; the *Policía Nacional* is a national anti-crime unit who wear a dark blue uniform; and the *Guardia Civil*, with green uniforms, is a national force whose most conspicuous role is as a highway patrol. Spanish police are generally very courteous and helpful towards foreign visitors.

Where's the nearest police station?	**¿Dónde está la comisaría más cercana?**

PUBLIC HOLIDAYS (*días festivos*)

Banks, post offices, government offices and many other businesses will be closed on the following dates. Andalusia celebrates its regional holiday on 28 February. Note that there are also a number of local and regional holidays and saint's days – check with the local tourist office.

1 January	*Año Nuevo*	New Year's Day
6 January	*Epifanía*	Epiphany
19 March	*San José*	St Joseph's Day
1 May	*Día del Trabajo*	Labour Day
25 July	*Santiago Apóstol*	St James' Day
15 August	*Asunción*	Assumption Day
12 October	*Día de la Hispanidad*	Columbus Day
1 November	*Todos los Santos*	All Saints' Day
6 December	*Día de la Constitución*	Constitution Day
8 December	*Immaculada Concepción*	Immaculate Conception
25 December	*Día de Navidad*	Christmas Day
Movable dates:	*Jueves Santo*	Maundy Thursday
late March–late April	*Viernes Santo*	Good Friday
late May–early June	*Corpus Christi*	Corpus Christi

R

RELIGION

Spain is a Roman Catholic country. Mass in English is conducted in Benalmádena-Costa, Málaga, and Torremolinos. Protestant church services in English are held in these resorts and also in Fuengirola. There are synagogues in Málaga, Marbella and Torremolinos, and mosques in Fuengirola and Marbella. For further details, refer to *Sur in English* (see MEDIA on p.121) or contact the local tourist office.

T

TIME DIFFERENCES

Spanish time coincides with most of Western Europe – Greenwich Mean Time plus one hour. In summer, another hour is added for Daylight Saving Time (Summer Time), keeping it an hour ahead of British Summer Time.

New York	London	**Spain**	Sydney	Auckland
6am	11am	**noon**	8pm	10pm

TIPPING

Since a service charge is normally included in hotel and restaurant bills, tipping is not obligatory. However, it's appropriate to tip bell-boys, filling-station attendants, bullfight ushers, etc, around 50 ptas for their service. About 10 percent of the bill is usual for taxi drivers, bartenders and waiters.

TOILETS/RESTROOMS (baños, sanitarios)

There are many expressions for 'toilets' in Spanish: aseos, servicios, WC, water and retretes; the first two are the most common. Public toilets are to be found in most large Spanish towns, but rarely in villages. However, just about every bar and restaurant has a toilet available for public use. The usual signs are Damas for women, and Caballeros for men, though you might occasionally see Señoras and Señores

TOURIST INFORMATION OFFICES (oficina de turismo)

Information on the Costa del Sol may be obtained from one of the branches of the Spanish National Tourist Offices listed below.

Australia: Level 2–203 Castlereagh Street, NSW, 2000 Sydney South, tel. (2) 2647966.

Canada: 102 Bloor St West, 14th Floor, Toronto, Ontario M5S 1M8; tel. (416) 961-3131.

UK: 57-58 St James' St, London SW1A 1LD; tel. (0171) 499-0901.

USA: Water Tower Place, Suite 915 East, 845 N. Michigan Ave, Chicago, IL 60611; tel. (312) 642 1992;
8383 Wilshire Boulevard, Suite 960, Beverly Hills, Los Angeles, CA 90211; tel. (213) 658 7188/93/95;
665 Fifth Avenue, New York, NY 10022; tel. (212) 759 8822;
1221 Brickell Avenue, Miami, FL 33131; tel. (305) 358 1992.

These offices will supply you with a wide range of colourful and informative brochures and maps on the various towns and regions in Spain. They can also provide listings of hotels and campsites on the coast, listing all facilities and prices. For more detailed information on destinations in Andalucía, contact the Andalucía Government Tourist Authority: Empresa Pública de Turismo de Andalucía, Edificio Eurocei, Autovía Sevilla-Coria del Rio Km. 3.5, 41920 San Juan de Ayanlfarache, (Sevilla), Spain.

Once in Spain, you will find official Tourist Information Offices in all the main cities and resorts; these normally open from 9am to 1pm and 4 to 7pm. All of them will have somebody who will be able to give advice and information in English.

TRANSPORT

Buses (*autobús*). An inexpensive and frequent bus service links the towns and resorts along the Costa del Sol between Málaga and Marbella, and Torremolinos has its own urban service. Less frequent buses will take you further afield, to Gibraltar (2 hours from Fuengirola), Algeciras, Sevilla (3½ hours), Córdoba (4 hours) and Almería (7½ hours). Full details of fares and schedules can be obtained at local tourist offices (see TOURIST INFORMATION OFFICES).

Trains (*tren*). A suburban rail service runs along the coast between Málaga and Fuengirola (including a station at the international airport), with trains every 30 minutes between 6.45am and 10.30pm. From the mainline (RENFE) station in Málaga, fast trains leave regularly for Córdoba, with connections to Sevilla, Granada and Algeciras. Timetables and information are available from railway stations and tourist offices. The mainline station in Málaga is on Calle Cuarteles (information, tel. (95) 2360202), west of the city centre; tickets and information can also be obtained at the downtown RENFE office at Calle Strachan 2 (off Calle Marques de Larios), tel. (92) 2213122.

Taxis (*taxi*). Taxis in Málaga have meters, but in villages along the rest of the coast they usually don't, so it's a good idea to check the fare before you get in. If you take a long trip, you will be charged a two-way fare whether you make the return journey or not. By law a taxi may carry only four persons. A green light and/or a *Libre* ('free') sign indicates a taxi is available. You can telephone for a cab: Benalmádena 2441545, Estepona 2802900, Fuengirola 2471000, Málaga 2351111, Marbella 2774488, Torremolinos 2380600.

Ferries (*barcos*). An overnight car ferry (departs daily except Friday) connects Málaga and Almeria with the Spanish enclave of Melilla in Morocco. Gibraltar and nearby Algeciras are major ports, with several car ferry, catamaran and hydrofoil services daily to Tangier and Ceuta in Morocco. The catamaran and hydrofoil crossings take only one hour.

Where is the (nearest) bus stop?	**¿Dónde está la parada de autobuses (más cercana)?**
When's the next bus/boat for…?	**¿A qué hora sale el próximo autobús/barco para…?**
I want a ticket to…	**Quiero un billete para…**
single (one-way)/ return (round-trip)	**ida/ ida y vuelta**
Will you tell me when to get off?	**¿Podría indicarme cuándo tengo que bajar?**

TRAVELLING TO THE COSTA DEL SOL

BY AIR

Scheduled flights link major European cities to Málaga's Aeropuerto Internacional, the main gateway to the Costa del Sol. There are direct flights to Málaga from London, Manchester and Dublin. Connecting services from cities throughout Europe and North Africa operate via Madrid's Barajas airport, which is the main point of entry to Spain for transatlantic and intercontinental travellers.

Charter flights and package tours provide the cheapest and most popular way of getting to southern Spain, but these tickets have certain restrictions which should be checked carefully before purchase.

From the UK and Ireland: You can choose from a huge variety of package tours, including accommodation and perhaps car hire, or opt for a flight-only ticket.

From North America: The Costa del Sol is included in some Iberian or Andalucian package tours that take in the main cities – usually Sevilla, Córdoba and Granada – as well as visiting the coast.

BY ROAD

From the UK, the main route from the French ferry ports runs south to Bordeaux and into Spain at Irun, west of the Pyrenees, then on to San Sebastián and Burgos. From there, you drive to Madrid and Bailén, continuing either south via Granada to the coast or southwest to Córdoba (then south again to Málaga) or Sevilla (and southwards to Cádiz). Allow two to three days of steady driving.

Alternatively, from Perpignan in south-eastern France, you can follow the motorway south via Barcelona to Alicante, continuing via Murcia to Granada, or Puerto Lumbreras or Almería.

Driving time can be cut by using the long-distance car-ferry service from Plymouth to Santander and Portsmouth to Bilbao in northern Spain (24 and 30-hour trips). From Santander or Bilbao, follow the road to Burgos and proceed as above.

BY RAIL

There is a direct but slow service from Paris to Algeciras. For Málaga, take the Paris–Madrid train, changing at Irun, and then the *Talgo* from Madrid for the Costa del Sol, a journey of 26 hours. Seat and sleeper reservations are compulsory on most Spanish trains.

Various discount rail cards are available. *Eurailpasses* are special rover tickets covering most of western Europe, available to non-European residents only, to be purchased before arriving in Europe.

The *Inter-Rail-Card* is available to residents of Europe. It allows either 15 days or one month of unlimited 2nd-class rail travel on all participating European railways in 19 countries, and is currently available for those under and over 26 years of age. The under-26 card can be bought for restricted zones of Europe at lower price (Portugal, Spain and Marocco constitute one zone).

The Eurodomino Freedom Pass allows unlimited travel on 3, 5 or 10 days in a month, in the country or countries of your choice.

WEIGHTS AND MEASURES (See also DRIVING on p.116)

Temperature

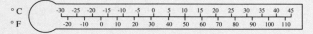

Length

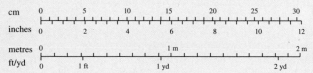

Weight

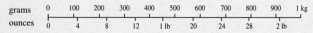

YOUTH HOSTELS (*albergue de juventud*)
(See also ACCOMMODATION on p.108 and CAMPING on p.110)
Youth hostels do exist in Spain, but they are few and far between, and not much cheaper than a room in a *casa de huéspedes*. Note that the Spanish word *hostal* does not mean 'youth hostel', but a certain type of hotel.

Index

Where there is more than one set of references, the one in **bold** refers to the main entry, the one in *italic* to a photograph.

136